slow food

ARTS & TRADITIONS OF THE TABLE

Carlo Petrini

Translated by William McCuaig

slow food

THE CASE FOR TASTE

 COLUMBIA UNIVERSITY PRESS   NEW YORK

Columbia University Press

Publishers Since 1893

New York   Chichester, West Sussex

Library of Congress Cataloging-in-Publication Data

Petrini, Carlo.

Slow Food : the case for taste / Carlo Petrini ; translated by

William McCuaig.

p. cm. — (Arts and traditions of the table)

Includes bibliographical references and index.

ISBN 0–231–12844–4 (cloth : alk. paper) — 0–231–12845–2

(pbk. : alk. paper)

1. Gastronomy. 2. Food habits. I. Title. II. Series.

TX631 .P474 2003

641.'01'3—dc21

2002191189

∞

Columbia University Press books are printed on permanent

and durable acid-free paper.

Designed by Linda Secondari

Composed by Audrey Smith

Arts and Traditions of the Table

PERSPECTIVES ON CULINARY HISTORY

Albert Sonnenfeld, series editor

Italian Cuisine: A Cultural History

Alberto Capatti and Massimo Montanari,

translated by Áine O'Healy

British Food: An Extraordinary Thousand Years of History

Colin Spencer

Contents

Foreword

I remember when in 1986 Carlo Petrini organized a protest against the building of a McDonald's at the Spanish Steps in Rome. The protesters, whom Carlo armed with bowls of *penne*, defiantly and deliciously stated their case against the global standardization of the world's food. With this symbolic act, Carlo inspired a following and sparked the Slow Food movement. Three years later, delegates from fifteen countries came together in Paris to pledge to preserve the diversity of the world's foods.

Since then, Slow Food has grown into a global organization that supports and celebrates food traditions in more than 40 countries worldwide. Slow Food has flourished in the United States as well. In the two years since a national office opened in New York, Slow Food convivia have sprouted in almost every state, and in this short time the U.S. membership has reached nearly 10,000.

Under Carlo's remarkable leadership, Slow Food has become a standard bearer against the fast-food values that threaten to homogenize and industrialize our food heritage. Slow Food reminds us that our natural resources are limited, and that we must resist the ethic of disposability that is reflected everywhere in our culture. Slow Food reminds us that food is more than fuel to be consumed as

Series Editor's Introduction

The New York Times, in a recent editorial entitled "Read This Slowly," asked its readers to "consider the Slow Food Movement, which took hold in Italy in recent years and is spreading around the world at an impressive clip."

Carlo Petrini, founder of the movement, here offers to our readership a consideration of Slow Food, its origins, history, and principles. At a time when globalization is a subject not only for debate but also for angry demonstrations in the street, this book is an important addition to the Columbia Arts and Traditions of the Table series.

There were 130,000 attendees, 80 participating nations, and more than 2,000 accredited journalists at the 2000 Salone del Gusto (taste show) in Turin, Italy. For the 2002 Salone, suffice it to say that more than 100 American food and beverage taste workshops (stands), 11 seminars, two Taste America dinners, and American embassy sponsorship constituted eloquent proof that Slow Food is effectively casting off its original Italocentricity for the many Americans who (to quote the *Times* again) "wish to wean themselves from the eat-and-run life."

The very name, Slow Food, originated in protest against the Golden Arches, that portal to the temple of fast food and to the caloric altar of its high priest, Ronald McDonald, who threatened to take over the plaza below the historic Spanish Steps in Rome in 1989. These birth pangs left the movement vulnerable to potential misunderstanding. Slow Food is *not* a gourmet food and wine society, though its meetings emphasize the rediscovery of the flavors and savors of regional cooking. The Slow Food Manifesto declares, "A firm defense of quiet material pleasure is the only way to oppose the universal folly of the Fast Life." Nor is Slow Food any longer a gastronomic movement, per se; it offers an antidote to the "insidious virus: Fast Life, which disrupts our habits, pervades the privacy of our homes and forces us to eat Fast Foods." In the name of productivity, Fast Life threatens to degrade the global environment and our local landscapes.

Here at the table lies the template for the preservation of human rights and the environment. TV chef Graham Kerr, formerly The Galloping Gourmet, now calls his program *The Gathering Place*. And Alice Waters has stated succinctly: "Eating is something we all have in common. It's something we all have to do every day and it's something we can all share."

Thus it was both predictable and normal that the manifesto's proclamation of the defense of slow, long-lasting enjoyment begin *at the table* with Slow Food; just as the original *table d'hôte* of the movement (thanks to the Internet) was in the small Piedmontese market town of Bra (near the heart of the white truffle and Barolo district). Slow Food quickly evolved into a defense team for vegetable, animal, and cultural diversity, taking the stand for animal and human well-being in its periodical *Slow*, now published in Italian, English, French, German, and Spanish. Its public face has become that of a primarily educational organization, which realizes that food consumption cannot be divorced from issues of food production and distribution; its mission is defined as "eco-gastronomic": for example, to convince the hygiene-obsessed EEC bureaucrats in Brussels, as well as the American public, that fresh produce is not dirty, though it comes without cellophane wrapping and looks unsymmetrical, and so unlike the waxen sterility of the processed and prepackaged products of the agribusiness industrial revolution.

The founder of the movement advocates creation of an *Aula* (Roman lecture hall) of Taste to bestow the Master of Food degree, a comprehensive and innovative syllabus of courses for a wide public. The curriculum would consist of 80 theoretical and practical lessons, with a final exam and a Master of Food Diploma. Since the 2002 inaugural sessions, 4,350 participants have enrolled.

Petrini and his disciples in their pedagogical offshoot Arcigola realize, however, that the educational process must begin with the young. The school garden is Slow Food USA's most notable activist undertaking, following in the furrows of the "edible schoolyard" experiment in Berkeley. There are Slow Food gardens (and chapters) in every major American city; these are also to become de facto seminars for children, experimental laboratories really, in sensory training. So, too, the American Institute of Wine and Food (AIWF) has as its principal educational mission an offshoot of the French government's *Semaine du Goût*, its successful Days of Taste program, wherein underprivileged youngsters are exposed to healthful cooking techniques, farmers' markets, and an initiation into savors and flavors.

Education is a slow process: farmers' markets have increased by 79 percent since 1994 to 3,137 markets in all 50 states; three million Americans patronize these markets. By their custom they may save the small farmer. But 40 percent of all U.S. farm income comes from government subsidies, and only 3 percent of our nation's farmers sell directly to consumers. Organic farms are still striplings among the sequoia of industrialized food conglomerates. And yet now, even amid the frenzy of globalization, the label ORGANIC occupies a niche in many supermarkets, especially in affluent areas.

The challenges for the Slow Food movement and its leadership are economic, political, and strategic:

Economic: Petrini inveighs against "the demagogy of price," emphasizing that we "must convince consumers to pay more for better products." But we already do! Compare the availability and high cost of produce at New York City's Union Square Greenmarket to those in supermarket chains in poorer neighborhoods. How to translate our espousal of Slow Food in nations with huge differences in disposable income levels, where obesity has become the visual manifestation of unhealthy lower-income eating, remains an ongoing dilemma and a growing concern.

Political: The perils of elitism—in the original 1989 international manifesto, Slow Food abjures "the contagion of the multitude who mistake frenzy for efficiency." *Odi profanum vulgus?* We cannot widen our membership base by disdaining that "multitude"; they are the army of consumers who may one day remove foodstuffs that embody quality, identity, variety, and taste from the endangered species list.

Strategic: While the movement has internationalized, its organizational structure (despite its English name!) still reflects a Turin *urbi et orbi* linguistic view. A chapter is called a *convivium* (plural, *convivia*); threatened artisanal producers and products are to be sheltered by the *Presidia*, helping them to publicize their foods. Endangered products to be saved from the deluge of standardization and macromarketing are to find refuge in the Ark. Taste instruction is at the *Aula Magna* of Taste. May I, though a professor of Romance languages, suggest that a linguistic delatinization of our movement is in order, in the interest of the universality that Slow Food aspires and deserves to achieve?

"The symbol of the Slow Food Movement and of the good life is the snail," *The New York Times* reminds us; I proudly wear my snail pin, the emblem of membership, on my lapel. Carlo Petrini's engaging book will persuade countless readers that time is the major seasoning of that good life, with a healthy table as the gathering place becoming the altar of a community pledged to "the delicious revolution."

Albert Sonnenfeld
December 2002

Slow Food is not just the title of this book. It is also the name of a
movement that today includes 31,000 people in Italy and 75,000
throughout the world. But it is also—and above all—an idea, or
rather a set of ideas. The most basic is our conviction that alimentation is an essential part of life and that quality of life is therefore
inevitably linked to the pleasure of eating in healthy, flavorful, and
varied ways. This is the opposite of what fast food is selling, with its
snacks and meals designed to be eaten hurriedly and distractedly,
their only virtues their immediate recognizability (thanks to standardization) and low price (thanks to standardization and inferior
quality). Slow Food, on the other hand, means giving the act of nour-
ishing oneself the importance it deserves, learning to take pleasure
in the diversity of recipes and flavors, recognizing the variety of
places where food is produced and the people who produce it, and
respecting the rhythm of the seasons and of human gatherings.

But the pleasure for which we stand is not pure hedonistic enjoyment for its own sake. On the contrary, the Slow Food "recipe" presented in this book is a proposal to wed pleasure to awareness and
responsibility, study and knowledge, and to offer opportunities for
development even to poor and depressed regions through a new

model of agriculture, as we have demonstrated working with our friends in Latin America and Africa.

Slow Food is a way of thinking shared by many people; here it is set out point by point. I have chosen to commemorate our origins and our first steps, and to tell the story of a group adventure that began with politics and wine and is now branching out to the Third World through prizes and Presidia, with the intention of promoting the choice and desirable things the countries there are producing, or could produce. The story is not told as an autobiography, though, or even the biography of a movement; rather, it is meant to sum up a current of thought into which my own reflections, and those of all who have worked to promote Slow Food, have flowed. Here you will find a portrait of our identity, not laws engraved in stone.

The book is divided into four chapters, each devoted to one of the four keywords and fundamental growth stages of Slow Food. First is the revolt against McDonald's and the birth of the movement; second, the effort to raise public regard for human and territorial resources; third, the necessity for the education of taste; and fourth, the campaign to safeguard plant and animal species and create markets for locally specific and traditional products. The appendix describes a handful of the Presidia we have created in Italy to safeguard traditional forms of agriculture and kinds of food.

I have tried to cover all our initiatives, not in order to please the participants and protagonists but to present a panorama of the strategic points at which we have concentrated our forces and the global reach of our project. In order to deal with the climate in which we are operating today, optimism and a few catchphrases are not enough; the alimentary history of the recent past is one of unsafe food and pervasive acceptance of the primacy of profit for the producer and savings for the consumer, summed up in the shameful slogan "low cost and minimal quality." The real remedies for the gastronomic ills of the twenty-first century are the assumption of responsibility for the future; the salvation of a heritage of memory, biodiversity, and creative capacity; and the affirmation of a pleasure principle that is the indispensable foundation for the strategies that we are working out as we go along. When we speak of responsibility and pleasure in the same breath, we can be certain that, if our full meaning is not immediately clear, at least we will get a favorable hearing.

This book is aimed first and foremost at those who do not know us yet. But it is dedicated to all those who have helped Slow Food to grow in recent years, as members of our Italian and foreign associations, in our Presidia, through our publications, and at the Salone del Gusto. Every page contains a bit of their work, their intelligence, and the pleasure they have found in sharing an idea and a practice. In countless convivial encounters, we have discovered "the case for taste" together. I hope to rediscover it with the readers of this book.

Preface to the American Edition

The story behind *Slow Food: The Case for Taste* begins in Italy. The idea for Slow Food was born in the mid-1980s in a small provincial town in the northwestern part of the country, on the edge of the renowned Langhe wine-growing district, in a social context that may be hard to grasp for those without a more detailed knowledge of life there at that particular moment in time. It was, in fact, in the local wine world that the movement started to grow, seeking to defend the "right to pleasure," which was increasingly being left by the wayside as the pace of life grew faster and foodstuffs more standardized.

The fact is, however, that it has always been possible to share the "case for taste" in every part of the world. Pleasure is a universal right, and the sensitivity and awareness toward food and drink that we have fostered over the years are valid everywhere. They are a world necessity.

As the number of Slow Food members has grown in different countries, so our story has been shared in all corners of our planet. At the moment, the United States is the country where Slow Food is developing fastest. This is significant, since it also happens to be the place where the industrialization of agriculture and production methods first spawned fast food. According to the cliché (and clichés invariably contain a grain of truth), America is a land where many people eat irregularly and mindlessly, simply loading up their bodies with fuel, often to the detriment of their health. No other country in the world has comparable problems of obesity.

I don't know if all this explains why Slow Food is now the second largest gastronomic association in the country. I don't know either if the trend toward uniformity of sensory perception, mass standardization, loss of identity, and unhealthy eating habits has been offset by a return to naturalness and the ability to appreciate flavors and smells—not to mention the pleasure of taking time to buy and eat healthy food. What I do know, though, is that the success the Slow Food philosophy is currently enjoying in the United States is symptomatic of new attitudes toward eating, living, and interacting socially.

We have entered an era dominated by globalization, hence by complexity. It has been said that globalization is an aggregate phenomenon with many facets, not all of them negative. The challenge now is to interpret these different facets and try to ensure that they make our lives richer in taste and also in satisfaction.

Taste, too, is a complex phenomenon, precisely because it is bound up with the most diverse aspects of our existence and our future. In this sense, Slow Food is also a way of coming to terms with the future of each one of us and of the entire planet. It's a challenge that we need to address with enthusiasm.

The Official Slow Food Manifesto

Approved by delegates from Argentina, Austria, Brazil, Denmark, France, Germany, Holland, Hungary, Italy, Japan, Spain, Sweden, Switzerland, United States, and Venezuela at the founding conference of the International Slow Food Movement for the Defense of and the Right to Pleasure at the Opera Comique in Paris on November 9, 1989.

Our century, which began and has developed under the insignia of industrial civilization, first invented the machine and then took it as its life model.

We are enslaved by speed and have all succumbed to the same insidious virus: Fast Life, which disrupts our habits, pervades the privacy of our homes and forces us to eat Fast Foods.

To be worthy of the name, *Homo sapiens* should rid himself of speed before it reduces him to a species in danger of extinction.

A firm defense of quiet material pleasure is the only way to oppose the universal folly of the Fast Life.

May suitable doses of guaranteed sensual pleasure and slow, long-lasting enjoyment preserve us from the contagion of the multitude who mistake frenzy for efficiency.

Our defense should begin at the table with Slow Food. Let us rediscover the flavors and savors of regional cooking and banish the degrading effects of Fast Food.

In the name of productivity, Fast Life has changed our way of being and threatens our environment and our landscapes. So Slow Food is now the only truly progressive answer.

That is what real culture is all about: developing taste rather than demeaning it. And what better way to set about this than an international exchange of experiences, knowledge, and projects?

Slow Food guarantees a better future.

Slow Food is an idea that needs plenty of qualified supporters who can help turn this (slow) motion into an international movement, with a little snail as its symbol.

slow food

Chapter 1

Appetite and Thought

The Origins

In Bra, a small city in Piedmont on the edge of the territory known as the Langhe, a group of young people were involved in social issues in the middle of the 1970s. They were connected with ARCI (Associazione Ricreativa Culturale Italiana), the national recreational association on the political left; their high level of activism was motivated by a strong cultural commitment; and they made their presence felt. Bra was undergoing transformation, but a century of industrial production had left its mark, shaping destinies and outcomes, urban landscapes and moments of repose.

> Our town was ringed
> by a belt of factories
> where blackened men scraped and hung hides;
> in the April sun the air smelled of leather.

quickly as possible and that, like anything worth doing, eating takes *time*. Slow Food reminds us of the importance of knowing where our food comes from. When we understand the connection between the food on our table and the fields where it grows, our everyday meals can anchor us to nature and the place where we live. And Slow Food reminds us that cooking a meal at home can feed our imaginations and educate our senses. For the ritual of cooking and eating together constitutes the basic element of family and community life. In short, Slow Food can teach us the things that really matter—compassion, beauty, community, and sensuality—all the best that humans are capable of.

It gives me great pleasure to introduce this volume to American readers. A revolution in the way we eat is taking tangible form in this country. There are farmers' markets in almost every city and the availability of organic food is expanding by leaps and bounds. In this book, Carlo Petrini eloquently articulates our mission, and I believe he will inspire more of us in this Delicious Revolution.

Alice Waters

We its citizens, every one, leaving here
bear within us a heaviness of stone
of thick fog and extracts of tannin.[1]

[Bra] has a heart that's been tanned
and left to dry in the sun
beneath the gaze of old gardens.[2]

The leather-tanning industry was created in the nineteenth century and was closely tied to the raising of cattle and the historical
presence of numerous clog makers and cobblers in Bra; it enjoyed a
boom during World War I thanks to orders placed by the military,
employing about a thousand people at its peak, but has been declin-
ing gradually ever since. At the period described by poet Giovanni
Arpino (whose mother came from Bra, and who lived there himself
for a long time and never lost his ties to the place) it still employed
two hundred people.

After World War II the production of tannin began in the city. It is
one of the basic substances used in the tanning process, and its pungent smell grabs the nostrils with an "odor that weighs down the air
like a thick dust and clogs your breathing with the stench of decom-
position."[3] Velso Mucci, a cultural and political activist and author of
the novel *L'uomo di Torino* (*The Man from Turin*), confirms that you
could never get away from the smell; he speaks of "a town where
the permanent gamut of smells runs from the great morbid stink of
rotting scraps of hide to the acrid sulphurous whiff of chemical tanning agents."[4]

But there are other smells that permeate the air of Bra:

the huge armpit of the town is pervaded every October by strong
exhalations of must that bring with them, from inside every

courtyard, whirling swarms of fruit flies. The people of Bra are making their wine. With a couple of tubs of grapes that they have harvested and dragged down from some tiny vineyard clinging to a steep hillside or hidden in a winding hollow of the clay hills, they all make their own wine at home.[5]

The same author gives us perhaps the best description of the town of Bra as it struggled along in the 1970s: "An agricultural economy based on small holdings, in an area passing jerkily through the artisanal and paternalistic phase of industrialization."[6]

Yet, along with pollution problems and a few handsome examples of industrial archeology, the age of tannin left another heritage: a history of workers' cooperatives that the socialist leader Camillo Prampolini called "exemplary" and a strong tradition of joining organized groups, whether Catholic, laic, or socialist in color. This tendency to form organized groups, called *associazionismo* in Italian, manifested itself as early as the nineteenth century with the formation of numerous occupational associations in agriculture, labor, commerce, the trades, and the military (until late in the twentieth century the concentration of barracks was another feature of the town). Of these associations, a few are still active today, like the Società di San Crispino e Crispiniano, which used to be made up of shoemakers and repairers, and the Società dei Contadini (Society of Peasant Farmers), the representative organ of the market gardeners, who were and are the most important component of the agricultural sector. Bra also gives its name to a cheese, although not a single round of this dairy product is produced in the city: it is actually brought in from the valleys of Cuneo, but traditionally it was the dealers in Bra who aged it and marketed it.

So all in all we are not talking about a gastronomic capital. Bra stands a little apart from the Alba basin, which is something of a destination for seasonal tourists and Sunday visitors; there one can find sleepy and little-known towns, and sample the variety of cultures that mingle between the Po and the Alps. Being born in Bra means having homemade wine from the courtyards of urban apartment buildings in your blood, not Barolo (the great red wine of the Langhe), but it also makes you sensitive to what it means to have a heritage of wine making, agriculture, and commerce. Having been born into a tradition of *associazionismo*, and having joined the ARCI ourselves, we wanted to compare this heritage with others from all over Italy.

This was the background of those who, in 1980, formed the Free and Praiseworthy Association of the Friends of Barolo, the nucleus of the future Arcigola. The promotion of wine and food, and thereby of tourism, was not a fashionable idea at that time and place, and there wasn't the faintest sign that this kind of tourism would become the great resource that it has. But that's what this unprecedented association was aiming at: to create awareness of local products and awaken people's attention to food and wine and the right way to enjoy them. And so we had our first tasting courses, organized sampling sessions and get-togethers, set up circuits for distribution, and began selling wine and specialty foods by mail order.

One of the most significant early events was held in the Palazzo dei Dogi, at Mira near Venice, in celebration of the wine and food of the Langhe. Massimo Martinelli from the Cantine Razzi led the wine-tasting, spoke about wine and vineyards, and told stories, and the Brezza family, owners of a restaurant bearing the family name in Barolo, prepared local dishes. The whole affair managed to combine information and pleasure in a way that characterized everything the group tried to do. Another case that comes to mind was a festive banquet organized for a meeting of philosophers at the University of Urbino by a couple of youthful founders of the association, Gigi Piumatti (today one of the editors of the *Italian Wines* guide and editor of the periodical *Slowine*) and Marcello Marengo: for perhaps the first time an austere citadel of high culture was permeated by the pungent odor of truffles, while the scholars, loosened by wine, reflected expansively on taste. Then there were the introductory courses on wine given to the students of the Itis Avogadro of Turin, and the Week of Barolo and Barbaresco held at Bra and modeled on similar courses given in Burgundy. Sheer willpower overcame a thousand organizational and economic obstacles to make these occasions happen, and through them we came into contact with people who, not long after, joined us to form the steering committee of Arcigola and then Slow Food. So the group began to grow as its own collective purpose turned into a search for a new identity. I myself, as a member of the national council of the ARCI, traveled throughout Italy in order to get to know its regions and its markets. But plenty of people do that without seeing the need for action and change: from Guido Piovene in the 1950s to the 1970s, those who made the "grand tour" of the Italian peninsula always took its geopolitical segmentation and its mosaic of regions as given, and considered the highly industrialized north and northwest (Lombardy and Piedmont) as the only model of development. But if you paid attention to material culture and thought about people's working lives and everyday routines, and the basic enjoyment of earthly goods, you began to see the enormous potential of Italy's agricultural and regional heritage, in terms of both its traditions and its economic potential.

Bra was still the laboratory for our ideas, and after the Friends of Barolo a cooperative was founded to help organize tourism and various sales and promotional activities. Next the Osteria del Boccondivino, a novel attempt to combine the atmosphere of a good restaurant with locally inspired cuisine, quality wines, and modest prices, opened its doors. The experience of working with ARCI, the organizational ability developed on the ground, the emergence of an operative base, and the building up of a network of contacts throughout Italy—these were the pieces of a puzzle. The pattern that emerged was of a group united by a shared interest in, and affinity for, cooking and the ways that food and wine go together. And in the space of a few years this little platoon and its scattered affiliates would become a worldwide association, attracting a membership interested in food and wine, certainly, but also in preserving agricultural and cooking traditions, keeping local products viable, and promoting conviviality.

On the organizational plane, an assembly of the ARCI at Abano Terme gave the go-ahead to a new federation that left full operational independence to the various initiatives that were taking shape in those years, ranging from Legambiente (the Environmental League) to the UISP (Unione Italiana Sport Popolare—Italian Sport for All Association); then in July 1986 the foundation of Arcigola gave the autonomy and the dignity of a "*lega enogastronomica*" (a "league for food and wine") to a structure that was already in existence and starting to coalesce. Our new constitution was celebrated over the course of two memorable days: first in the historic Tenimenti Fontanafredda at Serralunga d'Alba; then in the courtyard of the Boccondivino in Bra, with a dinner that only came to an end as dawn broke, following a last toast with a 1939 Barolo bearing the signature of Aldo Contemo; and finally in the castle of Barolo itself, at a meeting of the 62 founding members, who elected me president of the new fraternity.

The name "Arcigola" is a play on words: "Arci" comes from ARCI, but it is also a prefix meaning "arch-," and many founding members had a connection to the magazine *La Gola* ("*la gola*" = appetite for, enjoyment of, food; gluttony), so "Arcigola" suggests "ARCI-Gola," and also "archappetite" or "archgluttony." *La Gola* (1982–1989) was an original attempt to approach the culture of food and wine through disciplines like philosophy, sociology, literature, and anthropology. This monthly, published in Milan by an editorial cooperative, drew curiosity and interest from its inception and induced many people to attend tasting courses, come to social gatherings, and learn how food is produced.

For many isolated and curious gourmets, who were searching not just for wines and local specialties but also for a cultural setting and credible guidance, the arrival of the new association was a revelation: membership in Arcigola went from 500 to 8,000 in three years. This exponential growth was also fed by our publishing ventures, restaurant and wine reviews, organized trips and tastings, and discussion of ideas that would have sounded crazy a few years earlier, like slowness, taking things easy, and conviviality. The uniqueness of local foods everywhere and the concept of the traditional were suddenly being defended from a new point of view, by new groups of people.

In 1987 *Il Gambero Rosso* ("The Red Prawn") was born; this was a special insert dedicated to food and wine that Arcigola took part in producing for the left-wing daily *il manifesto*. Then came the idea of creating a guide to the wines of Italy; within a few years it became the reference book of choice for enthusiasts, producers, and restaurant operators.

With the launch of Slow Food Editore (Slow Food Publishing) in 1990, the movement gained an emblematic name and a powerful vehicle of identity. At a time when the restaurant trade was starting to suffer from the media's exclusive focus on places that were competing for Michelin's three stars, with scant attention paid to the kind of modest eating establishment traditionally called an *osteria* ("hostelry") in Italian, the guidebook *Osterie d'Italia*, the first volume in the Slow Food catalogue, took a stand against journalistic conformity and discussed the restaurant business using subversive terms like "tradition," "simplicity," "friendliness," "moderate prices," and above all "*territory*"—a word I will use throughout this book in exactly the same sense as the French word *terroir*: the combination of natural factors (soil, water, slope, height above sea level, vegetation, microclimate) and human ones (tradition and practice of cultivation) that gives a unique character to each small agricultural locality and the food grown, raised, made, and cooked there.

By 1989 the membership had reached 11,000, and Arcigola had been renamed Arcigola Slow Food. It became an international association as the level of communication among members and sympathizers, inside and outside Italy, rose and the rest of the world grew more and more interested. Why do we call it Slow Food? The name was coined when a number of our members took part in a demonstration against the opening of a McDonald's in the Piazza di Spagna, below the Spanish Steps in Rome. But what it really conveys is our critical reaction to the symptoms of incipient globalization (the term did not exist at the time, but "fast food" did). Slow Food became an international movement in December 1989 in Paris, where delegations from around the world met at the Opéra Comique to sign the *Slow Food Manifesto* reprinted at pp. xxiii–xxiv above. And that is how, in just three years, there came into being a worldwide movement aimed at gaining and spreading knowledge about material culture; preserving our agricultural and alimentary heritage from environmental degradation; protecting the consumer and the honest producer; and researching and promoting the pleasures of gastronomy and conviviality. Today Slow Food has 75,000 members throughout the world, and it is growing.

From "New Epicures" to Ecological Gastronomes

Gastronomy took hold among the aristocracy and the bourgeoisie thanks to its capacity to bring people together. Associations of food lovers go back a long way and take different forms. Some derive from the "tasting panels" of Grimod de la Reynière, who founded gastronomic journalism with the *Almanach des Gourmands* of 1803; similar panels were formed in Italy by Umberto Notari in 1929 in connection with the monthly *La cucina italiana*. Others originated as clubs combining bacchic revelry and poetry. In Italy clubs of this kind are indistinguishable in origin from the academies, and they sprang up in provincial towns everywhere as assemblies of (mostly male) people dedicated to the pleasures of wine, good eating, and conversation. Sometimes they were ephemeral, sometimes they lasted for a generation or so, but always they reflected a certain mentality, a certain epoch, a certain social class, and a certain economic context. In the twentieth century, gastronomic associations were also influenced by the cultural policies of the state: fascism discouraged them, except for the Touring Club Italiano, which dominated gastronomic culture during the twenties and thirties, but they revived in the Italian Republic after World War II as incarnations of the provincial spirit, fidelity to tradition, and a desire to bring back the rituals and feasts of the past. A taste for the scenic attached itself to gastronomy: costumes of dubious medieval origin and ceremonies of supposedly goliardic character were employed to enhance the fame of a particular kind of cured meat or a special dish. Reigning over all the other associations that sprang up in the wake of the postwar return to hearty eating was the Accademia Italiana della Cucina, founded at Milan in 1953, with branches throughout Italy. It was a gastronomic fellowship with a strongly marked social identity and cultural ambitions extending to the publication of guidebooks and collections of conference papers. Seen from outside, the Accademia was for VIPs and their substitutes, welcoming only people of the right sort and putting on show the appetites of people who had never been hungry in their lives. Though it was not overtly political, by the very nature of its membership it belonged on the conservative side of the political spectrum.

Born out of the diaspora of organized groups on the left, Arcigola and the team that produced the monthly *La Gola* belonged on the opposite side. Arcigola was created by a group of women and men who were born, and who live, in a part of Italy where people are raised to be able to talk about good wine and traditional local dishes, and who understand the way improved nourishment has redeemed the population from age-old poverty. The first people to call themselves "*arcigolosi*" or "archeaters" were an offshoot of that sector of 1970s political militancy that coalesced around the daily *il manifesto* and opposed other factions like the greens, the orange-clad followers of Bhagwan Shree Rajneesh, the marijuana smokers, and the vegetarians. Yet people on the left, no matter how sophisticated and modern they might be, had an odd relationship to gastronomy: eating well was something they did privately and unobtrusively, and they were mostly detached from and not much interested in the part of the economy that does grow and sell high-quality food, though a large part of the Italian population makes its living in this sector. This was the attitude taken by the leftist intelligentsia when Arcigola was launched in 1986: they looked down on us as a bunch of good-timers interested only in stuffing ourselves, while from the other side, the food and wine specialists affiliated with the Accademia Italiana della Cucina distrusted us left-wing gastronomes as incompetent intruders with an ideological agenda.

With ostracism coming from both sides—and flowing from a longstanding identification of communism with the spirit of Franciscan poverty—Arcigola immediately saw that it had to create an identity that would clear up that misunderstanding. The early members felt a sense of happiness and release as they laid claim to the pleasures of the table and the bottle, and they viewed conviviality as its own reward. An illustrative and amusing account of the matter was given by Enrico Menduni, a director of the ARCI, in the first issue of *Rosmarino*, the early and short-lived house organ of the association, under the title "A mezzogiorno qualcosa è cambiato" ("At noontime something changed"). Menduni charted the gastronomic history of a generation, and it was a choppy passage indeed, including rotgut wine consumed in *osterie*, cold cuts eaten at the Feste dell'Unità ("Feasts of Unity," the Communist Party's nationwide social gatherings), and tasteless food served in vegetarian restaurants, before the left finally made up its mind that "we want to eat well too."

Ironically, and with a healthy dose of playful spirit, we strange paladins used to refer to ourselves as "neo-*forchettoni*" ("the new epicures"), "*golosi democratici e antifascisti*" ("democratic and antifascist gluttons"), and "*nuovi edonisti*" ("new hedonists"), and for a while we had a mission to convert the entire left to good food and to pleasure in general. It was no accident that Arcigola showed up at the Feste dell'Unità in the summer of 1987 and organized a competition to recognize the best restaurateurs taking part in what was, at that time, the largest popular fair and family outing in Italy. We were convinced that to raise the quality of the food and drink served at the festival was a fit goal, as a matter of both politics and civility. Arcigola also took an active part, as I've said, in the creation of *Il Gambero Rosso*, the food section of *il manifesto*, in 1986. And, still within the ambit of the print media, it collaborated with the Communist Party daily *L'Unità* from 1988 to 1990, first through the columns of "AR," a supplement dedicated to tourism and gastronomy, and then in the pages of a section called "L' Arcigoloso" that came out every week for two years.

In 1994 the congress of Palermo approved the decision to go international, and in 1996, at the first Salone del Gusto at Turin, Arcigola

Slow Food opted definitively to combine ecology and gastronomy with the launch of the slogan "L' Arca del Gusto" (The Ark of Taste). Though we never ceased to affirm the cultural worth of gastronomy and the right to pleasure as indices of the quality of life, for a long time we still had to worry about justifying a choice that was often portrayed as purely hedonistic and a political retreat. Folco Portinari, an intellectual who took an active part in creating Arcigola and elaborating its initial ideas, invited the readers of "L' Arcigoloso" at Christmas 1989 not to trust either "moralistic revolutionaries" or "people who never laugh."[7] The task of the new association was to combine styles and notions that were thought incompatible until that time: excellent quality and affordable prices, enjoyment and health, delight in life's pleasures and social awareness, quickness and lazy rhythms. The purpose? To create an original and unusual social group that would be open, democratic, and uncontaminated by particular interests, and that would avoid making itself ridiculous with rites, protocols, and trappings.

The common identity of the members was strengthened by highlighting four major themes:

1. To study material culture, get to know about it, and spread that knowledge. This is the movement's principal theoretical and behavioral guideline: namely, that it is pointless to sing the praises of fine wine or the smell of good bread if you don't know how they are produced.
2. To preserve our agricultural and alimentary heritage from environmental degradation: the organoleptic profile of the food we eat (in other words, how it strikes our sensory organs) is being constantly impoverished. If that doesn't deserve high-quality production, what does? And then there is the artistic, historical, and environmental heritage of the places where we once bought and

ate food, like cafés, *pasticcerie*, bakeries, and the many sorts of shops run by craftspeople selling their own wares—all of them threatened by the invasion of fast-food chains and stores selling jeans.

3. To protect the consumer and the honest producer by letting people know, without rhetoric or bombast, where to find the right combination of quality and price, neither praising things that are good but expensive nor those that are cheap but substandard.

4. To research and promote the pleasures of gastronomy and conviviality, in a genial and tolerant manner that encourages an approach to food based on the hedonistic advantages of deeper knowledge, the education of the senses, and harmony around the table. In this sense the local representatives of Slow Food, the "fiduciaries" as we call them in Italy, or "convivium leaders," as they are known elsewhere (the term "convivium" will be explained below), should not be dedicated militants but people who seek gratification, friendship, and diversion.

November 1987 saw the publication of the *Manifesto dello Slow Food*, drafted by Folco Portinari and signed by myself and personalities from the world of culture, the arts, and politics like Valentino Parlato, Gerardo Chiaromonte, Dario Fo, Francesco Guccini, Gina Lagorio, Enrico Menduni, Antonio Porta, Ermete Realacci, Gianni Sassi, and Sergio Staino. It urged readers to "stop the fast-food virus and all its collateral effects" and made a "modest proposal for a progressive (in both senses) recovery of mankind as individual and species, and a clean-up of the environment so as to make life livable again, starting with the elementary pleasures." Arcigola embraced slow life, not just slow food, and in so doing it took its cue from *La Gola*; this magazine, created by Gianni Sassi and edited by Alberto Capatti, was the first real sign of interest on the part of Italian high culture in material civilization and the relationship among economics, ideology, and aesthetics. Arcigola Slow Food demonstrated to all and sundry that we were not just a bunch of people out for a good time, that we were dedicated to a project that would have an impact on everyday life and the way people function in the worlds of production, distribution, and consumption.

In 1991, the year of the second national congress at Perugia, the association emerged as a new phenomenon in the food and wine market in Italy. It brought together several tens of thousands of enlightened consumers, supplied them with publications, supported the education of the senses of taste and smell, promoted gatherings and large-scale events, and thus had enough weight to exert a considerable degree of influence on the market for good-quality food and wine. The convivium leaders and their collaborators became a cohesive team of operators in the area of food and wine around the country. Defense of tradition, enhanced appreciation for high-quality food, and knowledge of material culture underlay a range of initiatives that were really making a difference: for the first time mass education about nutrition was being accomplished with a light touch and in an agreeable way, favoring contact between producers and consumers and inventing original channels and methods for promoting their common interests.

Over the years the association grew. In the beginning we were militants of the left, tired and disillusioned, but as our activities and initiatives spread, other types of people were drawn into the orbit of Arcigola. Our tasting courses; our trips to the Langhe, Burgundy, and California; the publication of *Vini d'Italia* (Italian wines) at the end of 1987, the *Atlante delle grandi vigne di Langa* (Atlas of the great vineyards of the Langhe) in 1990, and the *Guida al vino quotidiano* (Guide to everyday wine) in 1992 brought the nascent community of passionate oenophiles closer to us—a group that was swelling along with the wine renaissance in Italy and attracting a whole subculture of young and enterprising producers. Arcigola Slow Food chose the snail, the symbol of slowness, as its emblem.

If there was a risk of becoming no more than a circle for wine bibbers, we evaded it by moving on different fronts. In December 1989, at the founding Congress of the International Slow Food Movement at Paris, Arcigola presented the *Almanacco dei golosi*, an inventory of the best craftspeople in food and historic places to eat out in Italy, in the tradition of the French gastronome of the nineteenth century, Grimod de la Reynière. In 1990 it was the turn of *Osterie d'Italia, sussidiario del mangiarbere all'italiana*, the first guidebook to eating places that offer good regional cuisine at moderate prices. These publishing ventures gave many food craftspeople, owners of *osterie*, and restaurateurs good reason to regard Arcigola as the best place to find out what was happening and what others were doing.

By now the overall intent and approach were well defined. The *"arcigoloso"* was an alert consumer, filled with curiosity, who wanted to take part at first hand and to learn; he or she frequented restaurants and wine cellars, shunned pseudoscientific presumptuousness and black-and-white pronouncements, respected the work of those who chose the food trades, and displayed tolerance. She participated in initiatives like the Fraternal Tables that undertake to bring aid to various parts of the world afflicted with war, famine, and poverty, because in the new millennium those who have grown, along with Arcigola Slow Food, to relish eating require two essential qualities: generosity and respect for the human environment. She is jovial and optimistic by nature and is able to communicate these qualities in daily life, and especially at meals: you can't enjoy good food and be greedy and ungenerous at the same time. Nor can you be a gourmet and not care about the environment: people like that wind up as dupes, exalting food and cooking that are clever but phoney. The project we call the Ark, launched on December 2, 1996 on the occasion of the first Salone del Gusto at Turin, sounds an alarm about the imminent loss of fruits and vegetables, animal species, and food products that form part of our collective memory and our patrimony of flavors. The project to found Presidia (see p. 93 below) responds to this threat by trying to resurrect older modes of production and revitalize local economies, pointing to a new way for world agriculture. So we come full circle: the new epicures have become ecological gastronomes.

An International Movement of Good Taste

Slow Food became an international movement on December 9, 1989 at the Opéra Comique in Paris, when delegates from fifteen countries signed a founding protocol signifying their adhesion to the ideological principles contained in the *Manifesto*; these focus primarily on quality-of-life issues in the widest sense, and on the harm that has been done over the centuries to our material culture. The founders pledged to respect individual cultural autonomy everywhere and to promote initiatives that will help and encourage people to get to know their own region and the things that set it apart better, while at the same time promoting active contacts leading to a better knowledge of, and appreciation for, the cultures of other regions.

The meeting at Paris, lasting from December 7 to 10, 1989 and including debates and dinners, tastings and gala evenings, was the end point of a long trajectory. From the beginning Arcigola had felt the need to escape the old habit of forming associations for purely municipal and corporatist reasons. The countless dining societies founded in Italy in order to enhance the reputation of the local wine, the local olive oil, or some traditional local dish were all provincial affairs destined to wither and die; on the other hand, the tricolor Italian flag had been reduced, by the beginning of the 1980s, to a worldwide symbol for spaghetti, pizza, mortadella, and Chianti in flasks. Neither of these was the road to the world of flavor we sought. Many factors signaled the need for a new approach, open to exchange and reciprocal discovery: the consumption of better-quality wine, the advent of wine and food tourism, the entry of new generations into the hallowed sanctuaries of quality production, and the new mobility and accessibility of food and wine themselves.

The Slow Food project was born in Italy in opposition to the fast food that landed on our shores and tried to take over, so the awareness that the issue was international was there from the start. The name we chose for our project, and the irony behind it, have caught on. Its force and its bite come from the choice of an English-language name conveying a stance that people all over the world immediately understand. In taking a stand against McDonald's and Pizza Hut, multinationals that flatten out flavors like steamrollers, we know that we have to fight our battle on their ground, using their weapons: globalization and worldwide reach. If fast food means uniformity, Slow Food sets out to save and resuscitate individual gastronomic legacies everywhere; if haste threatens the enjoyment of tranquil sensory pleasure, slowness is an antidote to hurry and the gulping down of nourishment; if the new ways of absorbing nutrition create stereotypes that trample local cultures, Slow Food urges people to recover the memory of regional gastronomic practices. If hamburgers are being consumed mechanically and giving the same stimulus again and again to the sense organs of the young, then we have to undertake a campaign of permanent education of the taste buds; if the places in which fast food is eaten are aseptic and nondescript, let's rediscover the warmth of a traditional *osteria*, the fascination of a historic café, the liveliness of places where making food is still a craft; if the handing down of knowledge about material culture from generation to generation seems about to cease as lifestyles and eating habits become industrialized, then let a new international movement keep the knowledge alive and tell people where to go to find it. If deranged habits of nutrition and fraudulently labeled foodstuffs threaten our health, then let's rediscover the well-being that comes from healthy food; if the invasion of agriculture by the chemical industry and senseless management of the land are menacing the environment, Slow Food supports growing methods that respect nature; if consolidation of the media is wiping out alternatives, the construction of an international movement fosters the exchange of information, analysis, historical research, and techniques of production.

Slow Food was born in Italy, but it does not speak for food and wine "made in Italy." On the contrary, the spread of the movement means receiving new input, mingling countless voices, discovering allies who think alike while respecting one another at a distance. It also means running the risk of misunderstanding and betting your trust on values like pleasure and quality that can vary enormously even within the bounds of Europe. But such a variety of people have joined or expressed support that Slow Food has become like a nerve center, getting and soliciting news about resources, products, and dining rituals that are universally enjoyable precisely because of their singularity. In order to learn how to find slow pleasure, one has to travel, read, and taste, abandoning the temptation of entrenched isolation: to eat a different kind of food in every street in the world is the best answer to fast food. Close to one another and yet distant, the members of Slow Food find their strength in this gift of ubiquity, but in a way radically opposed to what the media and McDonald's have to offer: slow culture is growing, it is heterogeneous but strongly cohesive, and it creates an elite without excluding anyone.

Being part of an international movement makes it possible to create real gastronomic identities that are not the result of ignorant fantasy or a media campaign; to practice cultural relativism in a sound way, learning and teaching that taste and distaste are the result of historical processes and cultural sedimentation; to overcome gastronomic chauvinism by incorporating diversities. Tradition, as a cultural goal, can only be recovered with a polycentric and multicultural approach of this kind. The magazine *Slow, messagero di gusto e cultura* (Slow, international herald of taste and culture) is the instrument of this project. We hoped and planned for a long time before it finally appeared in April 1996 in three editions, Italian, English, and German. With issue number eleven in September 1998, Spanish and French versions were added, and the magazine now speaks five languages. Its editor, Alberto Capatti, is an intellectual who has played a fundamental role in studying the history and development of nutritional culture in Italy; a large part of my personal education comes from him, and he has given the whole movement much greater cultural depth. *Slow* espouses a shared project that, by promoting the culture of food and wine, makes the profound recognition of diversity its foundation—diversity whose extent it does not want to reduce. In defiance of globalization, Slow Food recognizes the importance of identity, and of language as its principal component; defying all forms of conservative traditionalism, we are putting out a magazine of cultures, not of a monoculture. As we present, debate, revise, and translate our ideas, many of which were judged strange and obscure at first blush, they end up as part of the public discourse. Born on the Internet but printed on paper, written by collaborators from every country but produced in Bra, *Slow* is the cultural measure, as well as the organ, of the movement.

Pleasure Denied, Pleasure Rediscovered

> Let's admit it: the word "pleasure" still has a faintly dubious ring. A man devoted to work and raising a family is assumed to be an upright citizen, but a man dedicated to pleasure—you never know. Would you want your daughter to marry someone like that? We behave as though work and raising a family were proper and natural things, but pleasure we treat as somehow artificial, a luxury for a few—most likely undisciplined and shameless—people. Yet pleasure . . . is just as natural as, if not more natural than, work (which may itself be a source of pleasure for that matter), or duty and sacrifice, ideas that really are primarily determined by culture.

That was how Giorgio Bert began his article "Fisiologia del piacere" (The physiology of pleasure) in the July 24, 1989 issue of *L'arcigoloso*, and it was not the first time, or the last, that the pioneers of Arcigola Slow Food took a stand justifying and promoting pleasure. Indeed, the *Manifesto* signed at Paris in December 1989 was subtitled "International Movement in Defense of the Right to Pleasure."

Yet pleasure was, and is, a thorny subject: moralistic people feel itchy at the sound of the word; if you are involved in any sort of social cause or movement, your fellows will rebuke you for mentioning it; others will cite health concerns; and almost anyone will regard an interest in pleasure as a sign of superficiality. They all make the mistake of considering pleasure as synonymous with "excess." Hence the common prejudice (whether in good faith or bad). Above all, dedication to pleasure is theoretically impossible, for excess is simply incompatible with a steady routine. This is true in biology (our senses, for example, can become so accustomed to smells pleasant or unpleasant that we no longer perceive them) and in psychology too, for there is no form of pleasure that the passage of time will not make us take for granted or even dislike, no matter how lovely it may be at first. If habit blunts pleasure, then obviously we can't organize our lives around it. What is the consequence? Simply that in order to live pleasurably, we need to broaden the range of things that give us pleasure, and that means learning to choose differently, even to live differently. From there to gastronomy is an obvious step: alimentary monoculture (in other words, the restricted range of foods and flavors experienced by those who simply accept what is most easily available) blanks out the pleasures of the palate, because, no matter how much we like them, it makes them habitual. So embracing variety and difference really means performing an impossible trick every day—that of making an ephemeral and voluptuous pleasure last.

Next question: Is it risky for your health to make gastronomic pleasure a priority? If you look around you and think about models and codes of behavior, the situation we are in is a little like the Italian Renaissance, when the humanist Platina (Bartolomeo Sacchi) wrote his famous treatise *On Right Pleasure and Good Health*. Composed in 1465 and printed in 1470, this treatise on the art of cooking and dining helped to make his name and gained a following. Conservative and revolutionary at the same time, the work revived the medical concept of a personal "regime," rules for living based on profound knowledge of the body and aimed at achieving a balance between instinct and self-control, desire and wisdom, and—precisely—pleasure and health. Here is what Massimo Montanari wrote in *L'arcigoloso* for December 30, 1989:

The ideal of balance was the foundation of the philosophical, medical, and dietetic treatises of Greek and Roman antiquity, so it made perfect sense that this value system was revived by the culture of Renaissance humanism. For the humanists, classicism was a philosophy of life, as well as the philological study of texts.

Simple though it was, Platina's program was a genuine revolution against the cultural reality of the preceding centuries, for in the Middle Ages the classical ideas of regime, measure, and diet (in the literal sense of daily rules to be followed by individuals in order to optimize their health while enjoying life's pleasures to the full) had been undercut by ideologies and attitudes grounded in the contrary notion of "excess." Excess meant extremes of both abundance and deprivation. Food in the Middle Ages was a visible sign of wealth and power. Powerful men displayed their strength and fitness to command through their ability to eat and drink in large quantities. The opposite excess, extreme deprivation, was seen as a sign of perfection and saintliness: think of the ascetic practices of the hermit monks who mortified their own flesh through hunger in the belief that physical pleasure would lead them away from the spiritual realm and into sinfulness. The most insidious of pleasures, along with the closely related one of sex, was the pleasure of eating, or as it was called in medieval Latin, *gula* (literally "gullet," but used to mean "appetite for food" and so "gluttony," just like *la gola* in modern Italian), because no one could avoid it entirely. Once it got hold of you, you would come to appreciate it more and more, and it would pull you down. So the Middle Ages saw a proliferation of anticulinary techniques designed to cancel the sensory appeal of food and turn it into a tasteless, formless mass.

Pleasure was pushed to the outer limits of the range of positive ethical and cultural values, and excess took its place as a criterion for behavior. That is where the dichotomy between pleasure and health comes from. Health concerns overrode all else, and dietary science dominated the literature on food with the theory that everything people ate had to be justified on grounds of health. Food only had value from that point of view. Yet as Madame de Sévigné noted, "health is the pleasure of the other pleasures. If the other pleasures are all eliminated, one may perhaps live longer, but health itself will vanish along with them."

We are now half a millennium away from the Middle Ages, but all our modern schizophrenia does is keep the medieval philosophy of excess alive and make it worse. We still mortify the flesh when we sit down to eat, denying ourselves wine and tasty treats under the illusion that that will keep us perfect and immune. Food is pre-scribed like a "natural" pharmaceutical. But how natural can it be when it is completely cut off from all that differentiates one individ-ual, one region, one season, from another? Lack of attention to what's on one's plate is often a symptom of a broader mental out-look. Some people even maintain that a richly varied intake of food is economically unrealistic nowadays, or incompatible with the amount of time available. But monotonous eating is actually a recent and invasive phenomenon, related to consumerism and higher disposable incomes and the devaluation of food as pleasure. If anything, the opposite is true: less disposable income makes it almost compulsory to vary one's diet according to what is available. If you want proof, look at what people eat when they don't have much to spend, or what they eat in wartime. And then look at what people today are buying with the money they save on food: super-fluous possessions suggested to them by advertising campaigns, high-tech toys, designer clothing, and even worse, expensive med-ical and health-industry solutions—face-lifts, saunas, cosmetics, workouts—to problems originating with how they nourish themselves in the first place. Moralizing about how our bodies look, with all the tortures and deprivations that that entails, is a plague. As for the idea that nobody has time anymore, we have more free time than any generation in history, with our reduced working hours and long weekends.

The upshot of this ideology is widespread obesity in the very same western world blinded by the myth of perfection, a world where people eat industrially produced cookies, snacks, hamburgers, and carbonated soft drinks whenever they feel hungry, because that is what's easiest: quick bites, ideal for grabbing between one activity and the next, which you don't have to sit down and eat with other people.

Although from the strictly religious standpoint gluttony may still be one of the seven deadly sins, the real reason for this cannot be the pleasures of the palate themselves, but—once again— overindulgence. The most rigid theologian will confront an anomaly in the world outside the Vatican: nuns and parish priests savoring, with appreciative expertise, stuffed turkey at Christmas with a bottle of Barbaresco, and for dessert, panettone with a bottle of Moscato di Scanzo, in the quite correct belief that they are not sinning at all and are not the slaves of vice if they enjoy the same sorts of pleasure at every feast day in the calendar. It is all a question of measure and self-control. It is a sin to be intemperate, to throw oneself into a hunt for limitless pleasure. It is not a sin (indeed it is temperance, a cardinal virtue!) to enjoy wine and food as they are meant to be enjoyed. Not for nothing is the word *il bendidio* (God's abundance) a synonym for food in the Italian language.

The pleasures of the table are the gateway to recovering a gentle and harmonious rhythm of life. Go through it and the vampire of advertising will lose its power over you. So will the anxiety, conformism, and suggestive power of the mass media that the shifting winds of fashion impose. Let go of standardized, sterile models. Freedom to choose could raise the quality of life and bring pleasure within reach of large masses of mankind. To be able to sit on the terrace of a café without being poisoned by the exhaust fumes of automobiles; to visit historical cities at a gentle pedestrian pace; to stay in tourist attractions that haven't been ravaged by speculative overbuilding; to eat choice foods produced by local craftspeople. . . .

The answer to the environmental and existential degradation caused by the fast life will not come, contrary to what a certain late-yuppie ideology would have you believe, from searching even more intently for "quality," if that means an exclusive refuge for the elite from the madding crowd. Upscale patterns of consumption, quite apart from the ideology that underpins them, are no longer a defense against degradation, and paying top price no longer guarantees quality of life. A good example of this occurred at the end of the 1980s in the United States, where Perrier water had become an upscale item and a status symbol among those who had arrived and those who were scrambling to do so. When it turned out to be contaminated with gasoline, 160 million bottles had to be withdrawn from the market. It is true that people are drinking more bottled water all the time on account of the deteriorating quality of the tap water. But what sense does it make to import mineral water from the other side of the ocean?

Slow Food will teach you how to distinguish between one kind of quality and another. There is the kind we may call "hard," because of its huge environmental and energy costs. Quality of that kind could never be produced in adequate amounts, at least not the way it is presently conceived of and consumed. For example, if everyone wanted to play golf instead of being satisfied with soccer, or even with simply being a soccer spectator, there would be no way to provide courses for all of them. And then there is the kind of quality that Slow Food wants to promote, a "soft," renewable kind that improves quality of life for the largest possible number of people. The search for it may not free the world of all its unhappiness, but it will make it a much more enjoyable place.

McDonald's Versus Slow Food

Many people see Slow Food as the direct antagonist of fast food, especially McDonald's. This view would be true if it were not so reductive, and if we had ever mounted an explicit campaign against the king of the hamburger chains. The fact is that we have never fully linked arms with the angry crowds on the streets of Seattle and Genoa, or said, with José Bové, that "when a hamburger place springs up, Roquefort cheese dies." The French union leader who became famous for trying to block the spread of McDonald's in his country—in particular for the incident at Millau, in the south of France, that earned him some jail time—and who is today one of the leaders of the antiglobalization movement has voiced ideas that have often cast a spell over us. But when he adopts a strategy of direct action, he chooses a path leading to head-on confrontation with the multinationals, the path of the guerrilla fighter, that we prefer not to take. That is not the slow style. Our choice is to focus our energies on saving things that are headed for extinction, instead of hounding the new ones we dislike. But if you want to revive a tradition and give it fresh life, often what you need is a new toolkit and some avant-garde ideas. When we refer to "new agriculture," for example, we are not talking about some kind of rural archeology.

Since McDonald's is the leading symbol of the new American imperialism, let's take a closer look at its history in Italy, which simply mirrors its presence in the modern world and which it would be quixotic to try to ignore. The huge American chain had a hard time getting started in Italy, opening its first outlet at Bolzano in 1985, which was relatively late in comparison to the rest of Western Europe. Controversy exploded around the one that opened on March 22, 1986 in Piazza di Spagna, and there were other clamorous cases in which towns tried to keep them from coming in (Casamassima, a small community near Bari, drew national attention). When in 1995 it bought up a competitor, Burghy, from the Cremonini group of companies (about which we will have more to say in a moment), the number of McDonald's hamburger places in the Italian peninsula went from 33 to 142 overnight, and from that point on there was no stopping them.

McDonald's penetrated Italy with a strategy the success of which, if you analyze it, shows you where the antidote lies. In other countries it began in the outlying regions and worked its way toward the main city centers, but in Italy it took the opposite tack. There the major cities were the first to be offered the McDonald's hamburger, and it was the provinces that stuck to their *osterie* and the other public places they did not want to give up. The Italian market for McDonald's in the 1980s and 1990s was already "Americanized" or else deprived of other gathering places: adolescents looking for somewhere to get together, organized outings of schoolchildren eager for the myths and the thrills they had seen on TV, wanderers in the shopping districts, and city-center office workers.

Here is what Mario Resca, the president of McDonald's Development Italy from 1995, had to say in a booklet published in 1998: "We are McDonald's, the most famous brand in the world, and we intend to conquer Italy." And moreover, "To fight McDonald's will take an awful lot of money, and really broad shoulders."[8] Signore Resca is right, and Slow Food realized that fact perfectly clearly even then, when we were not an association with "broad shoulders" and the last thing we had was "an awful lot of money." To resist the colossus we turned to another pair of "broad shoulders," those of the Italian provinces. We went to the places where McDonald's couldn't get a foothold, awarding (and gratifying) the *osterie* that served traditional dishes with our snail symbol.

Others may take the fight to the streets; Slow Food has a different idea: to rescue eating establishments, dishes, and products from the flood of standardization. Today the hanging signs of the traditional *osterie*, eclipsed for years by sandwich shops and places serving nouvelle cuisine fast-food style, are returning once more to the neighborhoods of Italy, thanks in part to our efforts to promote them, our books, and our conventions. It is all too easy to confuse standardization with globalization. Globalization is absolutely desirable when it creates networks of communication among diverse realities instead of leveling them. It offers real advantages to poorer countries as long as they can escape the logic of "conquest" that only creates wealth in the colonizing countries by exploiting the resources of those they colonize.

But let's continue with our visit to a fast-food place. What is it we don't like about McDonald's? Mostly the food itself, along with the condiments, which are the same everywhere, despite the attempts of the giant chain to adapt them to local taste in every country it colonizes. It is all very well to claim that in Israel there are fast-food places that don't serve cheeseburgers and dairy products, that the ones in India don't use beef, that in Saudi Arabia they pause five times a day so Muslims can pray, and that in Italy they don't use cucumbers. But these are all countries in which no one ever dreamed of reducing the ritual of mealtime to biting into an insipid bun containing ground meat whose origin you know you'd sooner not think about, even if it is certified and traceable to its source.

The real quality of the food remains hidden; despite all the effort they make to convince us that a Mcmenu contains nothing but good Italian ingredients, the information supplied is disappointing and sometimes not quite correct. In 1998 Mario Resca claimed (and information made available subsequently on the Web site of McDonald's Italia backs this up) that by now over 80 percent of the ingredients and raw materials used in their Italian outlets comes from Italian suppliers, including Inalca (beef), Amadori (chicken), Star (frying oil), Eisberg Italia (vegetables), Coca-Cola Italia (beverages), Peroni and Heineken (beer), and La Giara (olive oil).[9]

Today the Star and La Giara brands are no longer included in this list, and the oil arrives in McDonald's "restaurants" in individual packages bearing a multinational brand. Let's not even discuss Coca-Coca Italia, which is obviously no more than a branch plant; the same thing goes for the beer. The result is obvious: there are no real Italian products, in the sense of things produced locally and differing from one region to another, behind the claim that "our suppliers are Italian," and the same thing holds true in the hundred and more countries around the world to which fast food has spread.

Inalca is one of the main companies in the Cremonini group, the one that sold the Burghy chain to McDonald's. All over Europe, Inalca owns herds of Holstein-Friesians, a breed of cattle originating in Holland and the Friesian Islands, and the most familiar dairy cow in North America; Inalca slaughters more than 200,000 of them every year. Holsteins are easy to recognize: they are the ones with the dappled white and black coats. In Italy the Holstein, which yields more milk than any other breed, has taken the place of dozens of native breeds that gave milk with different or superior flavor and protein content, which was used to make various kinds of cheese that are getting harder and harder to find. And that's not all, for Holsteins also pose a threat to our splendid native Italian breeds of meat cattle because of the scale on which the food chains operate. When mad cow disease, which (surprise, surprise) only affects Holstein cattle, broke out, breeds like Piemontese, Chianina, Marchigiana, Maremmana, Podolica, and Romagnola suffered unjustly from the fall-off in beef consumption and the ban on traditional cuts, although anyone familiar with the scrupulous care that small herders dedicate to their animals had very little reason to fear that their meat was less than wholesome.

But here's the main point: How are these Holsteins raised before being ground up into hamburger meat? First of all, they are pumped for three years so as to produce milk yields two or three times higher than the average, using intensive methods that would be enough on their own to undermine the claim to quality. Then, when their milking days are over, they are converted into a beef breed by means of a different (but just as high-pressure) feeding program to accelerate their growth, because more and more ground beef is needed all the time. In a few months they wind up in our Big Macs, complete with a certificate of origin identifying them as "Italian meat" from the Cremonini group. Not exactly what you would call an impartial statement of fact.

Now let's look at the chicken: Amadori does business to the tune of around 700 billion lire annually, supplying us with such delights as McChicken patties and Chicken McNuggets. That these birds come from Italy is not in doubt, and we cannot even claim that they are battery-raised. Their feet do touch the earth, but each one has virtually no room to move, and sometimes their feet are so atrophied that the animals would collapse under their own weight if they were let loose in the open. In 48 to 56 days the cocks grow from nothing to around 3 kilos (6.6 pounds) and the hens to around 2.2 kilos (4.8 pounds), eating feed supplied by Amadori and receiving repeated injections of antibiotics to keep them "healthy." The stress inflicted on them during this microexistence, the absence of "animal well-being," shows in the meat, from which you would never be able to get the kind of good stock you can from a mature free-range chicken. These are born, gain bulk, and are slaughtered in less than two months, while a traditional chicken takes at least five or six months to reach the same weight.

Eisberg Italia is the company that supplies McDonald's with the vegetables for the mixed salad that goes along with their hamburgers. It was founded in 1995 by Stefan Cserepy and has the capacity to produce 1,200,000 kilos (2,640,000 pounds) of salad vegetables annually, doing business worth more than 4 billion lire in 1997. Needless to say, we are not talking about organic, or even simply seasonal, farming here: tomatoes, lettuce, carrots, and cabbage are guaranteed all year round. This is not agriculture with a seasonal rhythm, it is an industry running at full throttle, and the last thing it has to offer is variety of either odor or flavor, from one week or one month to the next (see chapter 2). The risk from transgenic organisms comes mainly from the suppression of biodiversity and large-scale industrial monoculture.

Finally we come to the French fries, another staple of fast-food places everywhere. Originally they were prepared daily with fresh potatoes, but in 1966 MacDonald's began using potatoes peeled, sliced, cooked, and frozen in huge plants, which guaranteed that, like everything else served in any fast-food place worthy of the name, they tasted the same everywhere. How so? By using the right amount and kind of frying oil, which gives them their flavor. Until 1990 the mixture contained 93 percent animal fat, which gave the fries their characteristic taste, but criticism about the resulting high cholesterol levels (there was more saturated fat in a single gram of fries than there was in a whole hamburger) led to a bit of sleight of hand. The animal fat was replaced by vegetable oil, but the original flavor was kept by adding aromatic substances, mysterious additives of unknown composition that have become the lifeline of the food industry in an age like ours of frozen, dehydrated, and sterilized food (i.e., food robbed of its original flavor).

The nutritional balance sheet has yet another item in the debit column: the way the food is eaten in a McDonald's establishment. The raw fluorescent lighting, the uncomfortable stools, the shared tables, the cardboard containers all act as inducements to eating quickly, without chatting; it is like a visit to a protein filling station. The ritual of sitting down together to eat, with its attendant sociability and personal service (not to mention gastronomic values) is sacrificed to practices deriving from Taylorism (assembly-line methods). Many young people wind up preferring wine bars as places to meet, because the cheapness of hamburgers is not enough to make up for the loss of pleasure, as we shall see below. McDonald's couldn't help but notice this, and its recent advertising campaigns in Italy are built around a pretense of sociability, featuring birthday parties and family gatherings. This celebration of the old-fashioned extended family (a purely Latin phenomenon derided in the English-speaking world) is irrelevant, and apart from that, it is hard to accept birthday parties with French fries and dinners with smiling families guzzling soft drinks.

Notwithstanding all this, Slow Food is not against McDonald's just because it hates hamburgers and French fries and regards spending a long time around the dinner table as compulsory. A slow pace can sometimes become agonizing; who doesn't recall some terrible wedding banquet like that? Conversely, fast food doesn't have to be disagreeable, and there are some traditional ways of eating it—archetypes of McDonald's in a way—that we point to as customs worth saving in our guidebooks, like the *lampredotto* (a kind of tripe) ritually eaten in the *piazze* of Florence; or *pani ca' meusa*, the spleen sandwich of Palermo; or *morzeddu*, the bread stuffed with stewed tripe of Calabria. So it is not just a question of opposing slow to fast, but rather of highlighting more important dichotomies, like carefulness and carelessness or attentiveness and haste: attentiveness to the selection of ingredients and the sequence of flavors, to how the food is prepared and the sensory stimuli it gives as it is consumed, to the way it is presented and the company with whom we share it. There are endless degrees of attentiveness, which in our view are just as important whenever and wherever we take nourishment, whether it is a meal at home or in a restaurant, a drink in an *osteria* or a sandwich at a bar, lunch in a school cafeteria or in an airplane. The real difference in quality among these experiences does not lie in how much time is devoted to them, but in the will and the capacity to experience them attentively.

It is worrying that fast food has been able to capture such widespread and indiscriminate support among youth. That many young people like to eat that kind of food and drink that kind of beverage probably has something to do with a new attitude to nourishment, and a pricing policy that brings hamburgers within reach of every social class. But the fact that children and adolescents see fast-food places as favorite spots in which to meet and communicate (sometimes the only such spots, aside from discotheques) remains puzzling. Fast-food places are actually "immoral," if we think of the Latin root from which the word "moral" derives. *Mos* in Latin, with its plural *mores*, refers to the "customs," the universe of habits and behaviors to which a people conforms, although no law codifies them in black and white. Fast food, with its planetwide standardization, has swept away all these traditions, these *mores*, when it comes to food. Admitting for the sake of argument (although it isn't true) that consumers of fast food get as much pleasure from that as others might from savoring a glass of Barolo or gathering merrily around the dinner table—still, how is it possible to renounce the practices, the rhythms, the layers of cultural sediment that make up our history and our identity without running the risk of turning into barbarians? Adopting the same ancillary role that children's television programming does in the afternoon, fast-food places now organize and host children's birthday parties. In this they are given a strong push by the reduction in urban space suitable for play and the absence of carefully thought-out consumer alternatives. In a vacuum of political, civic, and family responsibility, quality is given up for lost. Even on the part of a public that cares about wine and cheese at dinnertime, a laissez-faire attitude persists toward the rising generations, who are left to their own devices. Let them stuff themselves with hot dogs and dribble ketchup everywhere; "when they're old enough the kids will develop a taste for Barolo."

The real mistake here is that we are favoring an inclination that doesn't belong to our history, in the hope that when they grow up, young people will recover their lost palates. But bad habits contracted in youth—the target age for fast food—rapidly become ingrained, and the upshot is a loss of identity, of the heritage of individuals and societies. And at the new McDonald's, opening soon, they are adding more seats all the time.

Chapter 2

In the Beginning,
the Territory

Cultivating Diversity

The foundation on which we have built Arcigola Slow Food is the concept of *territory* (regional and local specificity; see p. 7 above). Local
cultures are the answer to the drive to standardize inherent in the
fast-food model; their variety and diversity are the key by which our
members all over the world acknowledge and understand each other.
From them we get wine, raw ingredients, culinary techniques, histories, identities, and the habit of exchanging knowledge, products, and
projects. Territory seems like such a simple point of reference, but it
has its own history, and in Italy, Europe, and the world during the last
twenty years it has gradually changed, becoming something we need
more than we ever did, and also something more complex.

The first time we really grasped what a well-defined, coherent, and suggestive territorial reality could be was in France. Visiting cellars and restaurants in Burgundy, Bordeaux, Alsace, and Champagne in the early 1980s, we came to see that these territories were something more complex than what you could find in most of the Italian provinces. It is not just individuals or business enterprises with a plan that give the famous French vintages their mythical status, it is a certain idea of production combined with a communication strategy that makes it possible to "sell" the world a complex image combining history, landscape, wine, cuisine, and a style of welcome. This well-oiled system functions perfectly in a country like France, where wine has been made for two millennia and gastronomic pride is a common heritage, cutting (like the culture of good taste itself) across all the social classes. At a time when the reawakened demand for high quality in the wine sector, and along with it a more cultivated and aware restaurant industry, was just starting to be felt in Italy, we as Italians were struck by the way certain regions in the world had achieved exemplary production systems like the ones we saw in France, and were evolving rapidly. The extraordinary flowering of the new California wine industry, for example, represents a reality that we saw we would very soon have to confront.

Arcigola was born in an area with an ancient agricultural tradition and a splendid landscape, as well as some distinction in modern literature with Cesare Pavese and Beppe Fenoglio, and even a few artists of genius (although not well known at home or abroad), like the experimental avant-gardist Pinot Gallizio. Barolo and truffles are its signature products. The Langhe district was a sort of Burgundy in the larval stage, with much the same social and economic reality as its French counterpart (the vineyards are broken up into many small holdings, unlike in Tuscany), but its wines, despite their ancient pedigree and great distinction, were having some difficulty winning consumer acceptance. In the space of a decade, though, the rustic Barolos of the 1970s gave way to more elegant wines thanks to modern techniques of vinification and greater focus on the vineyards. Yet Alba and the surrounding territory did not have in place the infrastructure, and above all the mentality, to meet the demands of wine and food tourism, which was then on the rise and already starting to lure the forerunners of what would turn into a floodtide ten or fifteen years later onto the back roads of lower Piedmont.

So it was in the Langhe that we in the newborn Arcigola decided to try out our notion of "building" a territory, in the sense of an integrated system, an inventory of resources, a project dedicated to specific goals. On July 14, 1988 we summoned an estates-general of the food and wine industry in Langhe: hundreds of wine producers, wine merchants, restaurant owners, and journalists came together to debate the question "Could the Langa be to Piedmont what the Côte d'Or is to Burgundy?" For the first time, it was proposed that everyone work together on a large-scale project of image promotion, and make intelligent use of the region's natural advantages by overcoming the delays that were slowing the renewal of cellars and eating establishments. The publication of works such as the *Guida enogastronomica e turistica delle Langhe e del Roero* (Wine, food, and touring guide to the Langhe and Roero) and the *Atlante delle grandi vigne di Langa, il Barolo* (Atlas of the great vineyards of the Langhe, Barolo) still lay in the future.

The *Atlas* was a project on which a group of enthusiasts worked for years. Reprinted in 2000, when it was expanded to include the area producing Barbaresco wine, it was the first true catalogue of the vintages of the Langhe's noble wine, which have now been fixed forever (a need unmet by the local land registries). In order to compile it, the vineyards were measured, the oral testimony of old folk sought out, the histories of cellars and labels retold. It is a work that singles out, highlights, and values difference—the individual sections of each vineyard, the distinct characteristics of each vintage. It gives each of those pieces of ground, firmly identified at last, its own separate economic profile.

Other initiatives (described in detail below) were soon to follow, as we pursued our efforts to build an alternative model and enhance its value: "Agrarian Assemblies" to keep those engaged in farming up to cultural speed and "Wine Conventions" that drew audiences both curious and knowledgeable, forging a new bond among consumers, products and those who made them, and the territory.

Our association was founded on what we came to call "*Condotte enogastronomiche*" (literally, wine and food "practices," as one might refer to a doctor's client area), which straddled arbitrary administrative divisions and brought ancient local identities, with their own resources, products, and culinary traditions, back to life. A *Condotta* (which is called a "Convivium" outside Italy) is made up of a portion of territory and a group of members of our movement, who organize activities like social events, sampling sessions, courses to develop taste, and visits to producers. Each is headed by a democratically chosen "fiduciary" or convivium leader who coordinates these activities and maintains a link with national headquarters, taking part in our annual policy and strategy conference. Areas of Italy such as the Maremma, the Marca Trevigiana, Monferrato, Tuscia, the Val Tiberina, the Ponente Ligure, the Langhe, and Ticino have all come back to life in this way. Everywhere "cultural" roots are being rediscovered: olive and grape varieties like *taggiasca* and *barbera*, red *radicchio* and *scottiglia* (the typical mixed-meat stew of the Tuscan Maremma), *agnolotti dal plin* and *Verdicchio*. Every single product defines and shapes a space of its own, and together they make up a geographical mosaic with multiple intersections, where borderlines are traced by a change in the ingredients of a *sugo*, a different method of cooking, the presence in the fields and orchards of a certain grape variety or vegetable or fruit, convivial get-togethers and popular feasts. Italy is known as the land of a thousand *campanili*, but it is also a land of a thousand flavors. Thanks to taste and curiosity, it is as if it were reawakening from a deep slumber. Riches like these could only have been rediscovered and defended by an association like ours that expands by drawing nourishment from the resources of every individual territory.

At the Center, the Producer

In the beginning there was wine. It was the first of the daily foodstuffs to evolve into an item of luxury consumption, mobilize hordes of aficionados, make them want to learn more about it and organize their travel plans around it, provide fodder for newspaper columns, and generate a folklore about places and people. Yet it is impossible to tell the story of Arcigola Slow Food and its relationship to wine making without starting from a woeful time, the watershed scandal that drove many consumers away from drinking it and many producers away from adulterating it.

In 1986 quantities of wine that had been diluted with methyl alcohol in order to "create" a cheap drink caused the deaths of 19 people and poisoned hundreds of others throughout northern Italy. The epicenter of the earthquake was Narzole, a small town in the province of Cuneo where the Ciravegna firm, the one responsible for this criminal fraud, was located, and the shock waves spread through Piedmont first, and then through the rest of Italy and the world, causing exports to fall from 17 to 11 million hectoliters. In hindsight (and even without it), such a radical break with bad old habits had to happen sooner or later.

The methanol scandal, like the more recent ones involving dioxin in chickens and mad cow disease, arose from an ancient cluster of vices—downscale patterns of consumption and the drive for profit without regard for quality—that the Italian wine industry has since overcome. The calculation was shameful: methyl alcohol was cheap, and with it you could make wine that would sell at rock-bottom prices and still bring a handsome profit. Long before then the pioneers of Slow Food had begun to insist on ideas that would later become the guidelines of the movement, applicable to the whole wine and food industry: produce less and improve quality; consume less and pay a fair price (i.e., pay more) for quality. As remedies go, this one was blindingly simple, and the methanol scandal made it appealing. Obviously nothing justifies the loss of life; those who died were victims of a way of understanding agriculture and the work of country people with nothing but the rules of profit in mind. Remembering them today should make us wary of all those sectors of agriculture that are still controlled by large-scale feed producers, with farmers reduced to the status of assembly-line workers who, on their own farms, do no more than serve their livestock feed mixtures developed in the laboratories of the giant producers, with no respect for the well-being of the animal or the consumer. This is a subject to which we shall return; for now, let's go back to the story of wine and Arcigola, where we left them at the end of the 1980s.

Groups based in Bra and Rome (the latter previously with *il manifesto* and now with *Gambero Rosso*) were busy visiting the "prized" grape-growing areas, looking for the key to a new kind of quality wine making and struggling along as best they could without the tools to find out what they wanted to know. There was the Veronelli guide, valuable to the extent that it supplied the basic geography of Italian wine, but sometimes hampered by an insider approach and insider language. In France our basic manual was the Hachette guide, and we refined our knowledge by consulting Lichine, Johnson, and Anderson—the august elders of international wine criticism.

Then came in-depth tasting courses in Burgundy, Bordeaux, Alsace, Jerez, and the Napa Valley; and all the while we continued to investigate the world of wine within the Italian peninsula. The more we learned, the more we realized that the skills and the philosophy of production needed to be raised to new levels.

The Agrarian Meetings organized at Alba in the spring and summer of 1990 helped to meet this need. In both name (*Comizi Agrari* in Italian) and substance, these meetings were a revival of ones held in the late nineteenth century, following the unification of Italy, when qualified instructors traveled the country giving lectures and courses on the proper techniques for raising crops and livestock, bringing new levels of knowledge and awareness to the peasant farmer. One hundred years later, the producers of Langa were given a similar opportunity to meet the leading foreign experts in the world of wine. Speakers included Paul Pontallier, the director of Châteaux Margaux, and Billy Bonetti, the master of Chardonnay from California's Sonoma-Cutrer. The master of ceremonies, and indeed the illustrious patron of this unprecedented didactic initiative, was Giacomo Tachis, a leader in creating the wines that put Italy on the map of modern wine making (Sassicaia wine was the first and best known).

What we wanted to do was promote the message that the Langhe was an emerging area with the quality to rival the best France has to offer. Unfortunately, the obstacles did not vanish overnight: consumers with no standards on one side, and on the other wine snobs who turned up their noses at the native product, except for a few historic names plucked from a complex reality they had never bothered to get to know. Producers like Gaja, Giacosa, Bartolo Mascarello, and Ratti and the rising generation like Altare, Sandrone, Clerico, and Cigliuti are living proof that Piedmont is undergoing a revolution in wine production, with the great red wines of Alba attaining summits previously unknown, notwithstanding those on one hand who cling to a few faded glories, and those on the other who ground the ethics, and the good name, of wine making into the mud with their adulterated mixtures.

The Italian market was eager for information and responsive to it. Wine lovers were aghast at the fumes of homicidal adulteration rising from Narzole (in comparison to which the addition of sugar seems like a harmless piece of mischief) and were increasingly demanding reliability and quality. The small units of production in Piedmont, and the ones like them throughout the whole country, were ready to meet both requirements: their work was guided by the rules of their art, and quality was on the rise. The realization that it paid to produce good wine was like a crowbar, prying apart the baneful combination of bulk production and low prices.

But one piece of the puzzle was missing: an instrument to provide consumers with advice and indications about the most deserving wines and to make the best producers more widely known. The gap was filled with the appearance, in the autumn of 1987, of the first edition of the guidebook *Vini d'Italia*, published by Gambero Rosso in Rome with the collaboration of members of the Arcigola group from Piedmont (Daniele Cernilli and I were the editors). It was an innovative work, in terms of both approach and indications of merit. The 1987 preface contains insights that, fourteen years later, have proved to be correct, quite apart from the fact that many of the improvements urged have been carried out:

Apart from cases of fraud and adulteration, there is no legal norm that limits production (currently hugely in excess, with a surplus of 25 to 30 percent) or that gives the consumer any guarantee about the wine making processes used. "Table wine" is an expanse of ocean, with enormous tides of liquid worth very little, and small currents of wine of the highest quality that do not even fit into the doc [denominazione di origine controllata] category, because they actually exceed production standards in terms of quality.

As we noted, there were "a couple hundred rare pearls, but overall most table wine is truly disheartening." It was precisely against this background that crimes like the use of methanol were perpetrated. The latter was not just a lurid crime story, "it damaged the economics of the wine industry profoundly, penalizing excellent and honest producers, thanks in part to the virtually total absence of information for the bewildered and frightened public, who were certainly not helped to understand what was going on by most of the mass media." After noting that consumption per capita had fallen by more than 10 percent because of the methanol scare, we drew the bottom line, giving voice to hopes that have since come true:

> If this is going to mean drinking less in order to drink better; if the vineyards in the flatlands that (with a few exceptions) produce enormous quantities of poor grapes are all pulled up; if in the end we produce less, but better, wine that may cost more but that has unimpeachable characteristics of quality and genuineness, then it will be hard not to take some satisfaction in the fact that, although it was a terrible tragedy, the methanol scandal at least forced us to pull up our socks a bit. But if everything settles back down the way it was before, then there will still not be any controls in place, and consumer protection will still be entirely in the hands of the producers' sense of responsibility. If that happens, then there will still be a need for a guide like this, which, while it certainly does not purport to step in and do what the public authorities ought to be doing (that would be grotesque and ridiculous), can still give the consumer some sound advice and a few signposts through the enchanting chaos of Italian wine.

If we have gone from an initial print run of 5,000 copies to more than 100,000 copies in print today (with more than 25,000 copies each of the German and English versions), the analysis must have been on the mark then, and is still amply valid today.

The ranking system we invented in 1987—one, two, and for the best wines, three "glasses"—became so familiar to the general public that it is hardly proprietary anymore, while the guide itself is now copublished by Slow Food and Gambero Rosso (while the English edition is published by the Grub Street Press, London). A "three-glass" symbol indicates any superb wine, rare or not. The first edition of *Vini d'Italia* featured 32 "three-glass" wines, 500 producers, and 1,500 wines. The corresponding numbers in the 2001 edition are something of a miracle, considering that only a little more than a decade has passed: 230 "three-glass" rankings, 1,681 producers, and 12,045 wines. The criteria are as strict as ever, but so is our urge to keep in touch with the leading edge of wine production. All tastings are done "blind," without seeing the label on the bottle, and the entries give a description of every individual firm and analyze the flavor profiles of the most significant wines, avoiding the cryptic prose that is often used for that purpose and using instead precise and accessible language, readily understandable even by nonexperts.

The guide should not be seen as a mere marketing venture, an attempt to fill a publishing niche. The public with an interest in wine has grown in proportion to the quality of the wine and intelligent efforts to spread the news about it: without some instruction and a degree of methodical knowledge, 50 percent of the pleasure of eating and drinking well is lost. All the subsequent initiatives promoted by Slow Food, including the five great conventions held from 1990 to 1994, have stuck to this principle. These annual rendezvous, held in different places every year and at a time when Slow Food was not yet internationally known, each drew more than a thousand aficionados for three consecutive days, the majority of them foreigners who wanted to learn about, and taste, Italian wines from the regions chosen.

The first convention was held at Alba in 1990, and provided an opportunity to taste the best wines of Piedmont in cities, castles, and historical residences and visit the cellars of the producers, who spent three days showing the wine tourists about and hosting meals in their homes for small groups—ideal circumstances for gaining a direct acquaintance with the territory and its vineyards. The second convention, in 1991, was based in and around Florence and Siena, with excursions to the Chianti, Vino Nobile di Montepulciano, Morellino di Scansano, and Brunello di Montalcino zones. Many of those who took part still recall the wine-tasting staged in the Salone dei Cinquecento in Florence's Palazzo Vecchio, with the American participants gazing in awe at Vasari's painted ceilings or inhaling the fragrance of the rippling wine in their glasses and then imbibing it with a pleasure like that of a thief committing a miraculous heist. The third convention in 1992 was dedicated to white wine, so naturally everyone congregated in Friuli, at Gradisca d'Isonzo, in the Italian heartland of the Tokay, Sauvignon, Chardonnay, and Pinot Grigio grapes.

Our approach to wine took an international turn with the publication of the *Guida ai vini del mondo* (Guide to the wines of the world) in two editions, 1992–1993 and 1995–1996. Unlike the established guides, most of them compiled by English-speaking experts who travel from one place to another tasting and judging the wines of the five continents (and always attuned to an English-language readership), this one let the locals speak for themselves and be the judges of their own wines—an offshoot of the experience gained while compiling *Vini d'Italia*, for which there are tasting committees in the various regions. We never thought a guidebook should be a monovocal, centralized authority from which unquestionable verdicts emanate anyway. A guidebook for us is a relationship, maintained year after year between readers and authors, and its judgments are not absolute and beyond appeal but subjective and so debatable, and always expressed with a critical spirit and absolute honesty.

At the time of the *Guida ai vini del mondo*, Slow Food was present in 18 countries (today the figure is 83), and it seemed likely that the market for wine would become much more international within the space of a few years as patterns of consumption grew more varied, not only among populations that had recently discovered this beverage but also in countries that historically and chauvinistically consumed their own wine, like France, Italy, and Spain. Hence a source of information that went beyond the bounds of national production was needed, one that went into the different production techniques in the vineyard and the cellar in detail and described the variegated panorama of grape varieties and soils that give wine its character; a reference work that those engaged in the industry would find essential and that aficionados would find alluring. The *Guida* describes 1,900 cellars, comments on 5,000 wines, and, using the criteria described above, awards 150 wines the title of "top wine." It has been translated into five languages, with approximately 50,000 copies in print.

Lastly, Slow Food succeeded in creating a very special book, and thus bringing to completion a didactic project that began many years ago, when the first tasting courses were organized at the beginning of the 1980s. In the spring of 1993, *Il piacere del vino* (The pleasure of wine) came out, after a long and difficult period of gestation. The intention was ambitious: to offer, as the subtitle indicates, "a manual for learning how to drink better" of a new and modern kind, up to speed with the new teaching methods now in general use in the Italian school system (it is not a coincidence that the two authors, Paola Gho and Giovanni Ruffa, are teachers) and responsive to the needs of an ever wider public of ever younger adults with a curiosity about wine. The watchwords are seriousness of method and scholarliness in imparting information; clear and simple language; plenty of space dedicated to hands-on practice as a didactic strategy; and, instead of a provincial point of view, historically and geographically speaking, an insistence on seeing wine in the international dimension to which it properly belongs. Eight years later, five reprints and 50,000 copies sold are proof of the acceptance the volume has found among Slow Food members themselves (who use it as a textbook in tasting courses)—and not only them.

The reform of wine is, as I said above, only one battle being fought in a wider war for a new, high-quality agriculture, even if the charisma of wine is something special, even unique. When it comes to the literary celebration of eating—simple meals, copious feasts, or dainty sampling by aristocratic dilettantes—the finest pages, or at least the best known ones, would amount to very little without the rituals of wine, whether the drinkers are sampling or getting drunk, meditating or singing. Wine animates any occasion on which people gather to taste or to celebrate, with its rich historical and cultural heritage and the depth of its flavor profile.

If we approach taste in general the same way we approach the taste of wine, the challenge becomes greater, but the basic premise is the same as it was in the field of Italian wine in the 1980s. The rush toward industrial agriculture is starting to show its downside as the safety of food products becomes more doubtful. Conversely, the production of specialized local products is reviving everywhere, trust in organic food is growing, more and more farmers are returning to organic practices, and demand for choice, small-scale artisanal products is on the rise. Those interested in such products used to be seen as a niche market, but events like the Salone del Gusto at Torino's Lingotto facility (see below), with tens of thousands of visitors the first time it was held in 1998, 130,000 in 2000, and 140,000 in 2002, have shown that this market can no longer be considered a marginal phenomenon.

Consumers are divided and no longer fit neatly into categories determined by social class. The true dividing line is flavor and the importance one gives it. Some people see food as no more than nourishment, but others experience all its rich dimensions of health, hedonism, and culture. The problem, as we shall see, is not economic, for the percentage of their income that people spend on food today has fallen off steeply in comparison to the postwar period. Buying select products is not a question of cost, for anyone can afford better food by adjusting their spending patterns.

Now let's try to see things from the other side, that of the producer. If she has a real passion for her work, she won't allow herself to engage in economic competition with the large supermarket chains. She is playing a different game: to win gratification from the specificity of what she produces, from being "unique," from occupying her (yes) niche in the world of food production. This gratification is not purely economic: wine producers too are *contadini* (the Italian word historically implied "peasant farmers" and still carries that connotation, but the modern meaning is simply "farmers" or perhaps "country people"), yet today the names of some of them are pronounced with almost a fetishistic ring. Why should a herdsman or a sausage maker who produces a foodstuff of delicacy and refinement not receive the same reverence and esteem for the knowledge he has acquired and put to use?

The gap that opened up in the 1980s no longer has any reason to exist: there was a public of rich folk who consumed good food produced by poor country folk who got poorer the harder they worked, and there was a mass of people who consumed foods manufactured by the rich minority who owned giant and incommensurably powerful food industry firms. The work of those who lived on and from the land was looked down on, and rising generations, who saw in it neither satisfying economic prospects nor any moral gratification, were turning away. The project of Slow Food goes directly against this trend: food producers ought to be at the center of attention, to make up for the low esteem they have hitherto enjoyed, and rewarded for their work in rescuing a species of livestock, a fruit or vegetable, a variety of cured meat or cheese. This isn't just an Italian problem; it is the same in many other countries around the world, each of them a treasury of local specialties and individual traditions, a specific "heritage." If McDonaldization has succeeded all over the planet by offering the same meat patty to everyone, then others might achieve the same kind of expansion by emphasizing the culture of diversity and the fascination it can have for a gastronomically educated world.

The Rebirth of the *Osteria*

Slow Food's ideas about the restaurant business are just as radical: while the epigones of nouvelle cuisine continue to offer a gastronomic experience based on the decorative arrangement of the food on the plate, lightness, and experimentation,[1] our attention has been focused on the culture of the traditional *osteria*, promoting local identities, the proper use of raw ingredients, and the revival of convivial values and simple, seasonal flavors.

Osterie d'Italia, sussidiario del mangiarbere all'italiana (*Osterie* of Italy, a guide to Italian-style eating and drinking) came out in 1990; it was and is a directory of welcoming places to eat, where you can enjoy the dishes and wines of the territory you are in without being bled dry by overpricing or imprisoned in improbable fantasy settings. In opposition to those who would like to turn mealtime into a hasty pause or a ceremonial rendezvous, Slow Food sees the *osteria* as the symbolic locus of traditional cuisine, run as a family business, with simple service, a welcoming atmosphere, good-quality wine, and moderate prices. We are not museum curators, and it is not our intention to bring a dying breed of business tied to the rural society of the past (or the urban one, before consumerism) back to life. Rather, we want to give new visibility to a realm overlooked by literature and by the guidebook writers, a place that can still respond to the needs of thousands of consumers and reflect the profound changes that domestic and commercial cooking have undergone in modern Italy, with all the inevitable contradictions that entails.

The Slow Food team, coordinated by Paola Gho, searched the whole country to find and highlight the "everyday" places that conceal the soul of an *osteria* and keep the tradition alive: *trattorie* with home cooking, small urban eateries, taverns with a food menu, little country restaurants run by families, wine bars with a few hot dishes on offer, eating places attached to farm centers. Overlapping and hybridization make it difficult to imagine a strict catalogue of such places and hard to determine a set model to which they must conform. The old-fashioned *osteria*, now extinct, was a country gathering place and a kind of cafeteria/tavern in the cities; the new *osteria* is the place you go to meet friends in the evening, to eat with the family on Sunday, to pause for an hour at lunchtime and buy yourself a well-prepared hot dish and a glass of quality wine as an alternative to a sandwich or a cold buffet. We are talking about businesses with various profiles that carry out multiple functions and meet the typical needs and tastes of modern life.

Osterie d'Italia has redeemed these modest eating places, whether you call them *osteria* or *trattoria*, from prejudice and mistrust. Whether they are family operations, with flavor secrets handed down from mother to daughter and grandmother to granddaughter, or a handful of individuals with moderately conservative inclinations and the ability to manage a kitchen, wine cellar, and dining room, they are the antidote to the extinction of certain dishes. The culture of wine has given them a boost, especially where the owners belong to the new generation: quality bottles, decent glasses, competent service. And more than that: *osterie* show an increased concern with local ingredients and a search for artisanal products made in small batches. With the Slow Food guide, we can claim to have brought a hidden realm back to light, one ignored until now, or taken for granted, by other food guides, and to have provided a market for the many competent young people who are going into the restaurant business with modern attitudes.

Around *Osterie d'Italia* a movement has formed. The fashions that raged in 1980s Italy have passed away, and there isn't a kitchen, modest or renowned, that doesn't include some special dish or old-time recipe on its menu. The *osteria*—a name now seen frequently on the signs of new establishments—is enjoying a golden age, and everyone now makes "tradition" their watchword. What is traditional cuisine today? For many cooks, it means faithfully serving the old favorites. For others, it means rediscovering indigeneous recipes, oral or written, and trying them out in full awareness that they are linking up innovation with tradition. This "revivalism" is greatly preferable to all those improbable exercises in "designing" new dishes with tiny portions and no roots. If we take a step back and look at the actual ingredients of the recipes, tradition means primarily an attitude to the selection of raw ingredients: rib of beef, duck breast, and *carpaccio* must all be seen as the outcome of standardization that begins in the refrigerator and ends on the bill.

We have come full circle. Slow Food, which began with a crusade against the uniformity dictated by fast food, took a stand on the issue of our national style of eating out, making *Osterie d'Italia* one of the most highly visible tools in our toolkit and one of the most attractive—a guidebook like no other, that has turned an eating place from folk memory into a place where people are going today to appreciate the local territory and regional diversity. Every guidebook claims to help the reader pinpoint excellence; this one, though, is intended to be a *vade mecum* containing a portrait not only of the owners of the *osterie* but also of the reader: a person who, in daily life and at the table, displays a distinctive behavior in which curiosity, tolerance, awareness, openness, leisure, and competence join in harmony. A well-informed consumer, able to exert real influence on the way the *osterie* she goes to are run, as those in the business have grasped very clearly, by voting with her feet.

In the space of ten years, the new *osterie* have created a whole new category, now firmly established in a field (the restaurant business) where new sensations and the myriad of commercial temptations never end. If anything, the most successful ones risk becoming the "three-star" restaurants of the future. The growth in demand for local specialties and their popularity, the cult of wine and the ritual of drinking it, the availability of dishes that no one was making at home anymore and that restaurants ignored, might turn what began as a guide to eating out cheaply into a new *Michelin*. Who will safeguard the identity of the *osteria* as a place to take simple meals? The customers for one thing, as long as they stay faithful to constancy and quality, and Slow Food itself, as it keeps an eye out not just for quality but for the congenital vices of running any business.

The Difficult Voyage

When a territory has made all the right moves toward becoming better known, it has to defend itself against the success of its own resources, like the attractiveness of its landscapes, its cultural goods, and its gastronomic products. What if the exaltation of local special-ties provokes a feverish hunt to track them down, a cult of rarity and gustatory experience in and for themselves, apart from the histori-cal conditions in which they were once enjoyed?

This problem, unlike others to which Slow Food has forceful answers, is a tricky one, and it is probably easier to consider it in the form of questions without exhaustive answers, doubts that need to be talked through, and some thought about the heart of the dilemma: Is it better for people to travel or products to be shipped?

The easy answer would be that it is always better for people to travel: what is the point of exalting the differences between small segments of the land, as distant from one another as whole conti-nents, and then expecting that whenever a desire arises there should be a way to satisfy it right away and on the spot? The added value in local specialties lies precisely in the fact that their availabil-ity is restricted, whether by area or by season. It seems too obvious to need repeating. But if you start thinking about our modern ali-mentary habits, you soon realize that we are driven by appetites that demand immediate satisfaction by going to the nearest food store. Whether it is the season for them or not, there you will find strawberries in winter, pears in the springtime, apples at midsum-mer, and currants in the autumn. Somewhere in the world, less than twenty-four hours away by air, it is always the right season. Along with these eternal first fruits, we find cheeses and cured meats that seem to come from every corner of the earth (whether they really do or not) on the shelves of small stores and supermarkets.

But it is something of an illusion, this El Dorado. An economy based on massive use of transportation not only has serious environ-mental impacts in terms of energy consumption, pollution, surface congestion, and accidents but also has the problem of an impover-ished range of goods on offer. That range is dictated by "standards of quality" that steer consumers not toward local products but toward others formulated on the basis of desires induced by the media. Their allure, shaped by fashion, advertising, and in-store displays, and by the nominal qualities or supposed origins they boast, has to last just long enough to meet a fleeting consumer demand. The variety that greets us when we enter a supermarket is only apparent, because often whole sections are offering exactly the same thing. The differences lie in the packaging, or variations in the dosage of aromatic substances and colorants. The fresh fruit and vegetables are all the same size and color, and only a few varieties are available. There are some kinds of food that consumers cannot even buy anymore, as regional products vanish from the shelves. When the right season for enjoying Italian apples does finally roll around, they don't look much like the stereotypes that have been imposed on us: not as big, not as smooth, regular, and perfect. Or else they are exactly the opposite: smoother, more regular and perfect than the others, to the point where we can't tell them apart. You can bet that the use of genetic engineering will only make things worse.

Animals travel too, and if you have ever had a chance to see the dreadful conditions in which they are transported, it is enough to convert you to local consumption. The stress starts the moment they are loaded. Pigs, calves, and bulls that have never known anything other than stables and stalls in the course of their brief existence are suddenly exposed to dazzling sunlight and forced to climb a ramp into a narrow truck, driven forward by electric shocks, blows, and shouts. The animal's quite understandable panic attack is only the beginning of what it is in for during the trip. The sheep refuse to drink even at rest stops; the bulls follow their sexual instincts and try to mount one another; the calves can't find their usual drinking troughs; and the cows, after hours on the road, begin to suffer painfully distended udders. The animals contend with one another amid vibrations, drafts, noise, heat, lack of space, drivers pushing to keep on schedule, curves, heavy braking, traffic jams, interminable backups on overcrowded highways. The upshot, as Manfred Kriener wrote in *Slow* for April 1998, "is the notorious PSE meat: pale, soft, exudative.... In the frying pan the cutlets shrivel, turning into a hard mass that you can barely chew." There would certainly seem to be a connection between the cruelty of animal transport and the low quality of the meat. We have actually verified that this is the case by raising Piemontese cattle in conditions that maximize animal welfare: if the animal does not suffer, is not irritated or made fearful, and travels the shortest distances possible, the meat proves to be of much higher quality.

Having said all that about the standardization of consumption and the drawbacks of transportation, we still have to face the disasters caused by the feverish hunt for local specialties and the serious damage that an unregulated influx of gastronomic tourists can do to a territory. No one doubts that cases of Amarone ought to be flown to New York rather than huge numbers of Americans converging on Verona, choking the roads, the hills, and the cellars. But we still need to be careful that greater knowledge about the products of a given territory does not explode into a cult. Look what happened to *lardo di Colonnata*, a prized Tuscan cured meat: gastronomes sang its praises to the point that when tourists flood into Tuscany looking for it, they are fobbed off with mounds of imitations. When a product becomes a status symbol, it draws a horde of profiteers and hustlers, and suckers who are easy to fool. The kind of tourism that Slow Food promotes with its guides, its tasting tours, its gastronomic strolls is meant to be aware and well informed about the places visited: respectful, slow, reflective, and as distant as possible from the culture of "use and discard." To savor the special dishes that every land boasts means feeling for the tendons of tradition and interacting with a patrimony made up of people, landscapes, and monuments. No product can be plucked whole from the context of which it is itself a cultural expression.

Gastronomic tourism actually presents a double risk: for the host and the visitor. The worst fate that can befall a place is to become a center of tourism, with everything that that implies: *trattorie* selling stylized local specialties at inflated prices, impoverishment of the soil because of the erection of hotels that violate the landscape, pollution caused by the excessive number of automobile engines, and massive importation to make up for insufficient quantities of locally sourced ingredients. For an example of the last phenomenon, consider what the truffle fair at Alba has become: there visitors are guaranteed the opportunity to buy the prized tuber for a whole month. Illusory and false availability—all the truffles in Alba and the surrounding area would not be enough to meet the demand generated in a single day by the mass of tourists that swarm into the capital of the Langhe. So truffles are brought in from foreign countries, deceiving the consumers and doing a great disservice to the quality of the excellent Alba truffles, a genuine local specialty of which only the name now survives.

The question with which we began—Is it better for people to travel or products to be shipped?—is not meant as a paradox, and maybe the best answer is a prudent one: it is better for people to travel, as long as they move attentively, choosing their route with intelligence and seeking to acquire as much cultural stimulus as possible from the land in which they find themselves. That resources are limited, and that we have to pay a fair price to enjoy them, is something we just have to accept if it means that those willing to devote themselves to the work of producing basic foodstuffs can make a living without succumbing to the industrial ethos. And doing without may sometimes be an act of respect.

In a world dominated by hegemonic forces that are threatening to turn it into a desert, our agricultural and food heritage has become a significant asset, and we have to actively defend its authenticity and favor the development of the territories in which it is rooted. To promote knowledge of that heritage and grasp its manifold connections with the nature of human settlements and their artistic treasures, to savor its products without turning them into cult objects, is the only way to build a relationship with its guardians and rediscover serene conviviality.

The Salone del Gusto

The idea for a Salone del Gusto, or Hall of Taste, and its realization are central to the story of Slow Food, because they represent a shift of political strategy. The first one was held in 1996, and although it was a small and experimental affair compared to those that followed, it gave a glimpse of the features to come. Already this was an event that intended to do more than reproduce the tired formula of a wine and food fair, half small retail and half folklore. In a space of just 5,000 square meters within the Lingotto exhibition center at Turin, we created a show that turned its back on the usual kind of exhibition and focused instead on the territory, its products, and its artisans brought face to face with consumers.

The public had to buy tickets to get in; when they did, they found a large market of products produced by local artisans, all of which they could taste and buy. As well, they could taste wines from all over the world and visit the stands of federations and associations.

The main theme of the new cultural policy was the training of individual taste, mainly through the "taste workshops" that had already appeared at previous events and were here the featured attraction, with places booked well in advance. Essentially the "workshop" consisted of the supervised tasting of wines and food products, with the aim of learning how these commodities were produced and how to analyze their flavor profiles. The main ideas of the movement were also presented and debated, and the campaign for an Ark was launched: for the first time, Slow Food had the chance to speak, from an important media platform, about protecting local products, and to make its position official through an ambitious project intended to open new pathways of production, marketing, and consumption.

The first outing was so successful that we decided to make a major commitment to the Salone: it would be held every two years, and it would be a lot bigger the next time around. The Regional Authority of Piedmont, I am glad to say, was enthusiastic about the project from the first and gave us full cooperation. Our luck in find-ing a regional president like Enzo Ghigo, who deserves credit for hav-ing the foresight to believe in the idea at a time when we were not yet in the spotlight, was one of the basic reasons the Salone was able to grow and become as important as it has.

In 1998 our exhibition space grew to tens of thousands of square meters, more than 200 taste labs were organized, and more than 300 producers of high-quality local foods displayed their wares. Slow Food prepared a highly articulated program, with the aim of attracting as many visitors and as much public notice as possible, and the results, in terms of participation and visibility, were exceptional. The success of the Salone was visible proof that sociologists and marketing man-agers were wrong to claim that young people were wedded to fast food and that the only people interested in high-quality products were a minority of middle-aged, high-income, self-indulgent consumers.

The Salone of 1998 was a watershed that pointed the way to a profoundly innovative rethinking of the Italian agricultural econ-omy. It showed those who attended, and many others as well, that when it came to small-scale local food production, Italy had few rivals, and that this patrimony (for too long dismissed as no more than a niche) could command a significant share of the market. One hundred twenty thousand visitors—including many interested and well-informed young people—were prepared to line up at stands in order to taste and buy traditional balsamic vinegar from Modena or sausage from the cinta, a Sienese pig, and to pay *prosciutto crudo* prices for *lardo*. This had an electrifying effect on a food industry that until then had been unable to see the potential of this sector. Thirty-five thousand participants in the taste workshops proved that Slow Food was right: there was an urge in modern society to find out about the history of food products from near and far and how they become commodities, to engage in comparative tasting, to learn how to evaluate the sensory stimuli of foods and wines. In the wake of the Salone, the agro-food industry sat up and took notice of this reality and began to emphasize local origins and high quality too, making notions like territory, tradition, and taste central to new product lines and advertising campaigns.

The Salone of 2000 was even larger in size, consolidating the innovative elements of previous years, and drew an even larger attendance. The latent socioeconomic trend was finally emerging, and this helped to bring about a change in the orientation of Slow Food itself. It was at the Salone of 2000 that we introduced and legitimized the Presidia (described in chapter 4 below, and in an appendix) through which the association has begun to take an active economic role in its own right and promote ideas through commercial channels while steering clear of media spectacle.

In 2002, the leitmotivs of the Salone were the defense of biodiversity and education. The aim was to demonstrate how pleasure without knowledge is merely self-indulgence, that the Slow Food enogastronomic movement had truly become "eco-gastronomic."

Arguably the most revealing aspect of the ongoing transformation was the development of the Presidia project. In 2002, besides 130 Italian Presidia, 21 new International Presidia were also present at the Salone (see the appendix). Hence Guatemalan coffee growers, Irish wild salmon producers, and a Mexican native corn cooperative, to name just a few, were all given the opportunity to show the world what they are doing, how, where, and why. The results were highly favorable, with most Presidia stands selling out and many finding international buyers. Eric Schlosser, author of the best-seller *Fast Food Nation*, who attended, said, "This new century demands new systems based on biodiversity. Slow Food is the beginnings of this new ideology and I support it entirely." Vandana Shiva, one of the world's most vocal campaigners for biodiversity and the founder of Navdanya Seed Conservation Movement, was also on hand to launch the first two Indian Presidia (basmati rice and mustard seed oil).

The Salone also saw the inauguration of the Slow Food Foundation for Biodiversity, which, from now on, will monitor the Presidia project's progress. As its Statute states, "The object of the Foundation shall be to support and disseminate the culture of biodiversity as a factor of human, civil and democratic growth. The Foundation shall work to safeguard the personal right to pleasure and to taste, thus establishing a harmonious relationship with nature in compliance with the traditions and the economic, gastronomic and agroindustrial identity of the *terroirs* of each single country. The Foundation shall study and promote a new, different culture of development, of civil coexistence and of slow living, undertaking to disseminate quality products in compliance with the natural environment and consumer rights. The Foundation shall work to promote the study and defense of the food, farming and artisan heritage of every country, and to protect the typical characteristics and features thereof."

Slow Food also wants people to be capable of appreciating and evaluating the foods they eat; we believe that the generations of the future have to understand what quality food is and where it comes from. Hence the second central theme at the 2002 Salone: taste education. Besides the customary taste workshops, and teaching programs for children, the event also showcased Slow Food's Master of Food and University projects, stressing the importance of education and knowledge in generating a new agricultural model, maintaining biodiversity, and forging an organic link between gastronomy and agrarian sciences.

In conclusion, the Salone del Gusto, which in 2002 attracted a record 140,000 visitors, has emerged as a new form of "cultural" marketing, a thousand times more effective than a trade fair, both from the commercial point of view and in terms of the promotion of our strategic goals. While Italy has obviously been the first country to benefit from the initiative, the signals from abroad are also increasingly encouraging, with members of the food trade (chefs, artisans, wine makers, technicians) taking an active part at the single stands and workshops. The Salone's success with the international public (conspicuously present in 2002) owes much to the high prestige of Italian wine and food, but also—and more importantly—to awareness that the event is responding to new impulses from the agroindustrial marketplace: at a time when the application of the industrial model to agriculture has reached a point of no return, the only feasible solution is the revival of traditional models of farming that respond to the new demand for quality and respect for the environment. Originally a place to simply taste food products, then a center to redesign the very foundations of gastronomy, the Salone has now become a biennial meeting place for all those committed to thinking about and testing the food, agriculture, and environment of the future.

Chapter 3

Educating and Learning

The Praise of the Senses and the Paradox of Taste

Beginning in the 1950s, a powerful wave of industrialization and modernization swept over Italy. Historians, sociologists, and anthropologists have studied the effects of the passage from a rural society that had remained almost unchanged for centuries to one that closely followed the pattern of development of the richest nations, led by the United States. The changes in lifestyle, collective mentality, patterns of consumption, and even the landscape have been profound. And there has been an enormous transformation in the way we take our nourishment.

Until the Second World War, around 60 percent of the limited household budgets of Italians went toward the cost of food, although the average diet remained meager: fewer than 3,000 calories per day per capita, on average. The basic foodstuffs were cereals, milk, wine, and little else. Only at the end of the 1950s did the con-

sumption of meat begin to grow, at a rate that soon became exponential, going from 22 kilograms (48 pounds) per capita in 1960 to
62 kilograms (136 pounds) per capita in 1975. Italians were now eating more cheese, eggs, fresh fruit, sugar, and coffee, while the quantities of corn and rice consumed fell off, and that of wheat held sta-
tionary only because of the spread of pasta from its traditional
stronghold in the center and south of the peninsula to the north. It
was also at this time that the depopulation of the countryside
began: 15 to 20 percent of the population changed residence, with
many country people relocating to the coasts or the major urban
centers, leaving villages and hamlets empty. The sharecropping
farmsteads were abandoned, while agricultural businesses turned
to monocultures, erasing the mixed farming of the old estates, and
with it the autarkic production of foodstuffs.

Statistical research into Italian family budgets, carried out system-
atically by ISTAT, the national statistical agency, since 1952, pinpoints
the new tendencies and the changes in modes of nourishment that
resulted from the preponderance of the nuclear family, increased
purchasing power, the decrease in heavy physical labor, and the
entry of women into the labor market. Consumption was no longer
restricted to local produce or local dishes (the spread of pasta was
soon followed, for example, by the success of pizza), and thanks to
the greater ease of transportation, was soon globalized.[1] Advanced
techniques of preservation, including deep freezing (for centuries
the only options had been smoking, salting, and drying) made it possible to find "fresh" products anywhere, at any time of year, inde-
pendently of where they were grown or raised and what the season
was. The food distribution system ramified. The cooking styles of the
different territories were suddenly in peril, crowded out by a sort of
alimentary syncretism. So was family conviviality, which died in the
United States with the advent of the TV dinner and later the

microwave, as precooked and reheated dinners were eaten in silence before the blue glow of the television screen. Meals got lighter and more amorphous, and the number of them eaten outside the house, at cafeterias, snack bars, fast-food places, and restaurants, grew. Influenced by a new cult of health, the body, and the mirage of eternal youth, people began to follow diets that dictated their choices in the kitchen.

Clearly the changed relationship between contemporary man and food derives from the slashing of the umbilical cord that once bound the world of the peasant farmer to the world of consumption, the producer of food to the diner. In today's society, almost no one procures their daily wine directly from a trusted vine dresser/wine maker anymore, or goes to a farmstead to pick up a week's supply of eggs, a chicken, or a rabbit. Almost no one is personally acquainted with the baker who makes the bread she puts on the table, or the sausage maker who personally takes part in the butchering of pigs and the preparation of salami and other meat products, or the cheese maker who prepares cheese from the milk of his own sheep or goats. The small food stores and the *osterie* that were once to be found in even the smallest villages, and to which people went not only to get their provisions but to keep in touch with village life and meet their neighbors, closed their doors one by one, and in the cities the spread of the supermarkets (which now control 40 percent of the food retail business) is inexorably smothering the small retailers, with all that entails in loss of human rapport, direct selection of merchandise, and exchange of information and acquaintance. We now prefer to buy individual portions of prepackaged, presliced, and often precooked food, and opportunities to feel it, smell it, evaluate it, and compare it—in other words, to know what it is we are choosing and why—are growing ever more rare.

In this way we have lost touch forever with an immense heritage of wisdom relating to the cultivation of fruit and vegetables, the raising of animals, and the preparation of artisanal specialties and even traditional local dishes. There was a time when the family and the social milieu transmitted knowledge of foods, recipes, alimentary customs, and the recurring yearly occasions for special meals. Today this chain of transmission has been severed, and neither the schools nor other social institutions have taken its place. The result is that children and young people in our time (and many adults as well) have never seen a cow or a stable, the courtyard of a farmstead (Italian farms don't look like North American ones) or a wine cellar, up close. They identify the smell of an apple with a brand of shampoo, and imagine that fish grow in the rectangular shape of the "fish fingers" they consume battered and fried. Their tastes are formed by what the food industry puts before them, from French fries to snacks with soft drinks, and stark elementary flavors crowd out complexity and nuance.

Yet on the other hand, we see that this loss of roots has left a void, surreptitiously filled by spectacles of various kinds and ably exploited by advertisers in order to foist industrial products on the public with messages evoking naturalness, genuineness, the link with tradition, and local specificity. Then there is the flood of cookbooks spilling off the shelves of the bookstores and inviting consumers to rediscover "old-time cooking"; the profusion of local festivals and banquets dreamed up in order to celebrate specialties or recipes, many of them highly improbable or outright inventions; the multitude of cooking shows on television, offering an idyllic and historically false vision of the gastronomy of the regions of Italy. The massive and often ill-fitting use of terms like "traditional," "tipico" (i.e., specific to a locality), "genuine," and "territorio" (in the sense discussed and used throughout this book) indicates a spreading phenomenon.

When choices about what and when to eat are no longer suggested (or dictated) by tradition and social milieu, everyone assumes direct responsibility for what she eats, swayed by advertising, fashion, diet information, common beliefs, and personal tastes and distastes. In this situation, the strategy to follow is a large-scale campaign of consumer education, so that, despite the din of the marketplace, everyone will be in a position to choose a proper, healthy, honest, and enjoyable mixture of foods for himself or herself. We need to reconstruct the individual and collective heritage, the capacity to distinguish—in a word, taste.

The primary instruments that, when trained, can make it possible for anyone to choose an adequate and enjoyable diet are our senses. Slow Food endorses the primacy of sensory experience and treats eyesight, hearing, smell, touch, and taste as so many instruments of discernment, self-defense, and pleasure. The education of taste is the Slow way to resist McDonaldization. It is not so much a question of fighting a fundamentalist war against the spread of the hamburger as it is of informing, stimulating curiosity, giving everyone the opportunity to choose.

To train the senses, refine perception, restore atrophied dimensions of sensory experience—these are the objectives of Slow Food. By "voting with their feet," consumers can actually do a lot to signal to producers that quality matters. But quality, which is an ensemble of objectively determinable values, even when it comes to food, has to be discovered, then learned and codified. That means gaining the kind of knowledge that allows you to determine how foods and wines are produced, how they evolve and change biologically, how they are preserved, which ingredients stabilize them and which denature them, and what characteristics enable you to classify them. Follow this route and you will acquire the salutary habit of recognizing and assessing what it is you are eating and drinking, and the beneficial effects will surely follow: you will be more demanding and you will discourage the kind of production that relies on short-sighted and indiscriminate purchasing patterns by offering low-grade food. In sum, if quality is our right as consumers, then it is up to us to equip ourselves to recognize it and ask for it.

Clearly a correct approach to food and wine is a question of mentality, of one's overall attitude to life—an attitude that does not repress pleasure but searches it out, making choices in the light of reason, the attitude of those who know how to maintain close rapport with the roots of things, who recognize the importance of material culture and conviviality. Real knowledge, not just superficial impressions, or worse than that, pedantry, opens the door to real communication and the sharing of interests.

Let me put the paradox this way: no matter how important sensory awareness and knowledge of how food gets from the fields to our dinner tables are in justifying our choices about what to eat, the pleasure we get from dinner is not reducible to a mechanical process or an arithmetical sum. Our pleasure is shaped in certain ways by different factors, cultural and sensory, and differences in the societal context and personal history of every person. Precisely because the word "taste" applies to many forms of culture, including art, fashion, and elegance, when used in gastronomy it also absorbs a thousand nuances that can't be chewed and swallowed, and is charged with values that often have little to do with flavor.

Hence the difficulty of challenging a system of food production that makes consumption into a total behavior and the product into an absolute value, proclaiming *gusto, goût, sapore,* and *taste.* . . . If training people's taste buds were all it took to transform their nutritional intake, then the world would live in a realm of complete gratification, total harmony, and the perfect marriage of didacticism and pleasure. Unfortunately things aren't like that, and tasting is not enough. This paradox can be more clearly stated by looking at the origin of fast food, the Adam's rib from which Eve was formed, and with her the end of the earthly paradise. McDonald's was born when the company made choices that differentiated it, starting around the end of the 1950s, from drive-ins and bars and cafés with juke-boxes, associating its hamburgers with familiar and reassuring val-ues and making sure all the restaurants served the same food the same way and that the employees worked as a team. Perhaps it is not an exaggeration to say that in the soft bun and the ground meat patty, the commercial strategy is so forceful that it is the dominant flavor. Against an adversary like that, classically ceremonious tasting sessions with just the right shape of glass and starched white nap-kins, as fragile as one's own taste buds, will make little headway and could never be the sole vehicle for launching a process of recovering memory and creating new conviviality.

Taste is a pact of fellowship and a program of cultural integration. It should be studied like a restless creature that thrives on diversity, works retroactively to revive memories, and goes forward blindly, promising virtual pleasures. It needs people who speak a Babel of languages and continually discover new foods, babies who grow up and, one day, hand on their own way of experiencing pleasure to other babies. Yet another paradox: in a world organized around hamburgers, popcorn, and French fries and reeking with the smell of deep-frying oil and deodorant, taste represents a new moral impera-tive. It signifies rigor in choices about production, even before choices about consumption, firmness in defense of our heritage against fleeting and heedless satisfaction. There is not a single Slow Food project that doesn't link pleasure with responsibility and food with awareness, that doesn't bring to mind a philosophical banquet in which eating and debate about the resources and values of the human race go hand in hand. Just yesterday we were talking about specific territories, about kinds of grapes and vegetables that needed protection, and tomorrow we will take up the destiny of a world that is called "Third" and is being culturally exterminated.

These paradoxes lead to very stark choices: if pleasure is a moral right, then an education and an ethics of taste become necessary and indeed indispensable for its attainment. This holds true for adults as they play the role of schoolchildren during one of our workshops dedicated to bread or olive oil; but the main target of this education will have to be the young rebels who prefer McDonald's French fries to homemade ones and are satisfied with the cold, overcooked pasta served at the school cafeteria. The philosophical banquet must speak about the kids, indeed *to* the kids. How Slow Food arrived at this contradiction requires a bit of history.

In the Schools

Slow Food, which has had a good many teachers among its members right from the start, was always aware of the need to measure its own ideas about the education of taste against those of the world of youth. Children and young people are the adult consumers of tomorrow, but their relationship to food is determined in the early years of life. In the past the early training of taste depended on generational models, modified by personal experience. Today the gastronomic tradition has been flattened and absorbed by the food industry, which targets the foods it markets very precisely to specific age groups. American kids smear peanut butter on their slice of bread, European ones smear cheese or salmon spread on theirs, and both of them wash it down with a drink that ends in "-cola." There was a time when every family's table, rustic or rich, bore the imprint of a distinct identity in the way the ingredients were mixed and cooked, but today we devour objects that come already assembled. A hamburger (bun + ground beef patty + cheese + toppings) is composed of ingredients that are precooked, compatible, and stackable. You can buy one in any fast-food place, and you can purchase the individual components yourself in any supermarket if you want to make one at home. In this way, domestic nutrition and eating out become mirror images of each other, and both increasingly depend on the same industrial source, which dictates what and how we eat.

Given this situation, it is a matter of urgency to intervene in the early years of life, when tastes and distastes are formed. This is difficult terrain, often overlooked by the school system itself, which in Italy is reluctant to deal with the topic of nourishment in its own right. Looking through the school curricula, you will find that, in relation to this topic, the legislation assigns two particular tasks to the schools: instructing the pupils in the facts about the life cycle, the human body, and its requirements, and the nutritive elements and how the body takes them in; and training them, in other words, promoting behaviors that will allow them to manage their body properly and keep it "healthy." The general rubric under which these tasks fall is "health education," and it is taught by the science instructors. So along with the habitat of the whales and the synthesis of chlorophyll, the science teacher also delivers lessons on proper nutrition. There are plenty of projects aimed at stimulating the students to think, do research, and learn, and teach them attitudes and behaviors. So we find course segments on the harm of tobacco addiction, the effects of spending time in discotheques, bodily expression. Unfortunately, amid the medley of experiences the schools provide, with outside support from psychologists, sexologists, doctors, nutritionists, and dieticians, we catch barely a glimpse of the fundamental concept that ought to underlie all these projects: that of "feeling good," with oneself and with others, achieving somatic and libidinal equilibrium. In the schemes for alimentary education, the black-boards are filled with tables, graphs, calculations of ideal body weight and the necessary quantities of calories, the physiology of nutrition, lists of foods that are "good for you" and "bad for you," and their nutritional values. The average student tends to equate this information with all the other information presented to her during the school year, and the clever ones take it in as a sort of "ought-to-do" that is in conflict with what their mothers serve at home or what advertising tempts them to eat. It never seems to occur to anybody, least of all the experts, that all this emphasis on alimentation might be connected with pleasure or the awakening of the senses of touch, smell, and taste. Although the school system is beginning to free itself, however slowly, of the idea that the body is inferior to the mind, there is still a need for a different approach to alimentary education, emphasizing the cognitive capacities arising from sensory experience and the need to bring children and adolescents to an awareness that begins with their own perceptual apparatus and arrives at a recognition of the qualitative characteristics of what they are eating, and the pleasure it can give them.

Slow Food has watched closely the experience of France, where in 1994 the Minister of Culture, Jack Lang, launched an event entitled the "Days of Taste." During this event, cooks and artisanal food makers took over the classrooms, telling the students about their professions and showing them the rudiments of a correct approach to food. This project got off the ground thanks to the Institut Français de Goût, set up in 1976 by Jacques Puisais, which plays a part in the French school system because of the strong conviction in France that taste is a mul-tisensorial message, made up of the visual, olfactory, chemical, tactile, and auditory stimuli imparted to us by what we eat and drink. Hence it is a medium of communication and a source of culture and convivi-ality. It lies at the origin of early childhood development. The awakening of the senses and the acquisition of a correct language and knowledge of the land and the seasons are its watchwords.

In June 1992, Slow Food launched "Taste Week" in Italy. It was organized on two levels. On one hand, we organized a series of presentations in the schools (compulsory and optional), during which people involved with material culture (cooks, pasta makers, sausage makers, pastry cooks) got the youngsters involved in supervised tastings, and gave them some hands-on experience as well. The classrooms were turned into workshops and kitchens. At the same time, the best restaurants in Italy threw open their doors to everyone twenty-five years of age and under, offering them a low-priced menu—a unique opportunity for them to catch a glimpse of the world of haute cuisine and the culinary art. Slow Food's initiative culminated in May 1997 with a gathering at Rome entitled *Dire fare gustare. Discorsi, progetti, esperienze intorno all'educazione sensoriale* (Speaking, doing, tasting: Ideas, projects, and experiences regarding sensory education), a meeting that brought all that had been achieved into focus and provided a national launching pad for one of the main themes of the philosophy of the movement.

In 1998, in the wake of these school programs for children and young people, Slow Food Editore published *Dire fare gustare, percorsi di educazione del gusto nella scuola* (*Speaking, doing, tasting: Projects for taste education in schools*). The Slow Food style, here and in other cases, is for the book to come out after, not before, the practical experiment has been tried. Our books are born of sensory experiences that need to be consolidated and expressed in words.

The author was Rossano Nistri, a primary school teacher long active in the field of sensory education and a constant presence in the activities undertaken by Slow Food to develop taste. The text reviews and organizes the teaching practices worked out over the years, and is presented as a tool for teachers (for whom courses to upgrade their competence in this field have since been instituted), but also for parents, who so often feel perplexed and helpless when faced with the eating behavior of their children.

Nistri meets the challenge of creating experiments centered on the use of the five senses, constructing a precise and systematic didactic manual, an educational project bolstered by techniques capable of reawakening and reordering the perceptual process. The teaching methods expounded are centered on the pleasure principle, a pleasure deriving from the knowing use of the senses, from learning about and handling raw ingredients, from rediscovering conviviality. Learning the sensory alphabet, then constructing the grammar and syntax of taste allows the student to come to an understanding of the cultural values tied to alimentation and the concept of local specificity. Thus food is linked to history, to social processes, and mentality, and the alimentary *imaginaire* is enriched, transcending the simple idea that eating is just swallowing. In the end, the children, the adolescents, and the teachers will have the tools necessary to select pleasures, tastes, variety. It won't be so easy for them to flounder in the chaos of the fast life; they will be a new type, ready to defend themselves against attacks on their own senses and improve the quality of their own lives. Aware consumers will come into being.

From the Workshops to the Master of Food

Slow Food gave concrete form to the idea of permanent sensory education with the taste workshops first introduced at the Vinitaly exposition at Verona in 1994 and offered many times since throughout Italy and abroad. The workshops were born of an intuition: to confront a human being with a food product. A workshop is neither a luncheon nor a menu; it is not even a single dish. It is a chance to examine a food or a beverage carefully, in a setting divorced from everyday eating rituals, and see them for what they really are: an olive, a wine, a cheese, each taken separately, one at a time. Participants learn to judge the flavor experience critically and become aware of the sensory impact of the food. They are seated at tables, like schoolchildren, and the atmosphere is that of a classroom, not a picnic. The direct approach becomes a formative experience, in the course of which expert practitioners of material culture (vine dressers/wine makers, cheese makers, pork butchers/sausage makers, pastry cooks, keepers of wine bars, restaurateurs) take the teacher's place, turning on their heads the traditional roles dictated by an ideology that has always placed the body and its needs on a lower plane than abstract thought.

During the workshops, which are not set up like a panel of experts and are not meant to be scientific in the strict sense, the participants scrutinize, sniff, taste, acquire information on how the substance in question is produced and enters commodity circulation, compare similar products, and try out unusual combinations. The class works together to acquire the vocabulary of flavor, learning the established one when it has already been codified, as in the case of wine and to a certain extent cheese, or creating one of their own, in cases (the majority) in which there exist only generic definitions. The workshops are a return to the senses and the analytical spirit, against the authority of books and merchandise, newspapers and advertising. In the workshops, taste in the truest sense of the term is developed: pleasure that evolves into knowledge and knowledge that turns to pleasure. The success of the formula demonstrates how the new gastronomic culture embodies a strong didactic thrust, aimed at getting to know food, and a demand for discipline, to bring order to the disorder of what is commercially available.

The next step is the Master of Food, which, of all the initiatives undertaken by the movement, represents the most impressive marshaling of forces and organizational capacity. In the course of a year, more than 1,000 teachers and coordinators are involved, and more than 30,000 members attend the lectures. The courses include, on average, three to six gatherings, and the course content deals with the processes of production, locally specialized and traditional products, the commodification of food and beverages, animal species, and the varieties of fruits and vegetables. Twenty courses are enough to endow the students with a comprehensive knowledge of Italian alimentation.

For some time we had noted a growing demand for knowledge of this kind, not only from the professional world but also from large numbers of consumers. The widespread fear caused by the wretched criminal actions of some producers heightened the desire to find out about foods and their provenance and learn how to identify quality. This demand is destined to grow in coming years, and the task of associations like Slow Food will be to meet that demand with methods adequate to lifelong learning.

Our courses do not mimic university lectures; instead we try to reconcile sound scientific content with an accessible style of presentation capable of holding the interest of participants, many of whom have not been in a classroom for a long time. The transmission of this kind of knowledge, which took place spontaneously in peasant society, is one of the prerequisites for reforming our way of life. The rise and the spread of ignorance about food is a social plague the opens the way for the most reckless fraudsters and hinders the growth of a renewed, aware agriculture. Unfortunately, those in government do not always grasp the problem, leaving the food industry to regulate itself—an industry whose entire raison d'être is increased volume. Only when the costs of this policy become clear are remedial steps taken. If the conviction does not take hold that alimentary education is just as important as learning to read and write, it will be impossible to plan the development of nonpolluting resources and defend biodiversity and our gastronomic heritage. If it does, the 400 current Master of Food instructors are no more than a small avant-garde platoon of a much larger army of teachers. The diffusion of alimentary culture will give space to the new generation of consumers, who, curious and passionate, will be able to make a difference in the way food is produced.

The present era is, sadly, characterized by widespread ignorance about agriculture and the environment. Proof of this lies in the absolute inadequacy of the debate on GMOs (genetically modified organisms), which, in the absence of complete answers from the scientific world and comprehensive ethical guidelines, leaves us wavering between rejection of this branch of applied research and blind faith in the new biotechnologies. Slow Food maintains that a new environmental conscience has to come about, with education playing a primary role. The success of nationwide courses in Italy must gradually be extended to other countries where the movement has gained a foothold. As this initiative spreads, it will lead to increased international exchange and the pooling of various experiences.

Many will ask how it is possible to reach such ambitious goals with the resources of a small movement like Slow Food. But it is the malleable and articulated nature of Slow Food that will make the project a reality. Our organization is used to intervening on the ground, arousing interest in high-quality production and modern production techniques. Along with our Presidia (see the next chapter), the Master of Food represents the backbone of our strategy, the concrete instantiation of a cultural policy that actively supports the new agriculture and works to develop a large-scale educational effort that is the foundation of the historical alliance between producers and consumers. This concrete utopia will bear fruit in coming years, when tens of thousands of Italians, fortified by the knowledge they have gained, will orient their shopping patterns toward high-quality food products with close links to the land, obtained through environmentally friendly techniques.

Presidia and Master of Food projects are destined to consolidate a role in civil society similar to that of the Agrarian Assemblies and Wandering Professorships (*Cattedre Ambulanti*) in the early years of the twentieth century—noble institutions that did much to raise the living conditions of the "rural plebs" who then amounted to more than 60 percent of the labor force. Today rural agriculturalists represent less than 7 percent of the Italian work force, and the corresponding figure in Germany and the United Kingdom has fallen to around 3 percent—telling figures. They don't have much bargaining power or electoral weight, and without firm alliances, they will not be in a position to accomplish the transformation that is needed. The leadership of the agricultural organizations itself has difficulty thinking otherwise than as a trade union; most of their demands are aimed at defending policies of government support for agriculture that have already done a lot of damage. If it is alliances that are needed, these will have to be sought among consumers, and not through "high-level talks" but through a direct relationship and a pact of mutual respect: high-quality production for consumers who know the value of agricultural labor and are willing to do their part for a healthy agricultural economy by paying fair prices.

The value of the Master of Food lies in the reply to the following question: Who is actively working to develop alimentary culture? Certainly not the schools, who in this respect are champions of apathy; not the scientific and academic hierarchies, which are more responsive to their own research interests and the needs of big industry; not even the noble sisterhood of nutritionists—useless vestals of an abandoned religion—or the print and television media.

If our Master of Food policy finds other associations willing to collaborate, it is not far-fetched to predict that new directions in consumption and new alliances may come about. If within a few years there is wider public knowledge of how cheese is made; of the native species of cattle and goats; of how yeast works in bread and wine; of how good prosciutto and salami are produced; of nonpolluting biotechnologies and organic growing; if all this leads to a new generation of cultivated and curious consumers, alimentary education will become permanent, and our labor will not have been in vain. Just as the agricultural calendar sets a time for seeding and a time for harvesting, today we are planting the seeds of a process of regeneration that demands patience and purposefulness: the harvest, we truly believe, will be abundant.

The University

The idea of setting up a center of higher studies in gastronomic sciences was born at the end of 1997, when plans were being made to renovate the Agenzia di Pollenzo, an agricultural estate on the borders of the Langhe. The size of the immense central building, once a royal residence of the house of Savoy surrounded by fields and watercourses, makes it possible to house a number of organizations, all connected to the effort to heighten appreciation of the territory and the great wines of the Langhe.

The idea of working to create a genuine university dedicated to the teaching of the gastronomic disciplines took shape. Toward the end of 1999 the Piedmont Regional Authority, in whose territory Pollenzo lies, took an interest in this idea, and so did the Emilia Romagna Regional Authority, which put forward the idea of transforming a former summer residence of the Farnese family at Colorno, near Parma, into a university center. An accord between the presidents of the two Regional Authorities made available resources, space, and housing.

A scientific committee has drafted a teaching program and carried out a feasibility study on the two venues and their suitability as campuses. A three-year undergraduate course is foreseen, in which future gastronomes will be given basic training in a range of disciplines including history and anthropology, the agrarian sciences, and sociology and economics; two years of specialization will follow, with two main options, one in the science of gastronomic communication (journalism, publishing, teaching), and the other in enterprise management (food marketing, the restaurant business, tourism). In addition, there will be a one-year master's program and extension courses on the Internet. Short courses to upgrade the skills of professionals in fields like the wine business and public administration will also be offered.

This is a novelty in the field of postsecondary education. Whereas food sciences and technologies are taught in the faculties of agriculture and veterinary sciences, and nutrition and diet are the appanage of medicine, the historical, cultural, and linguistic aspects of alimentation have never found a secure institutional home in Italian or foreign universities. The future University of Pollenzo and Colorno, as it will probably be called, will privilege a humanistic orientation, and for just that reason will be in a position to pilot the renewal of an important division of the human sciences and establish cooperative links with other universities around the world.

Gastronomy is one of the disciplines that the state universities of Italy have always neglected. Official culture has never accorded recognition to the study of food, except in connection with science and technology. But if we look at Europe and the other industrialized countries, we find ourselves on the brink of a revolution in education, and knowledge of food is of increasing interest in historical, linguistic, and anthropological research. In areas like food safety, the development of an agriculture aimed at producing high-quality products, and the certification of their historical and geographic origin, the demand for suitably trained people has been growing, not just in the technical sphere but also in sectors employing graduates with general degrees. Gastronomy is a clandestine presence in the training programs in fields like tourism and advertising, but it is not unrealistic to imagine that it will soon be taking its place in a larger framework of interests and objectives. The Pollenzo and Colorno campuses will together be the first center offering a course of gastronomic studies from a humanistic standpoint, a meeting place for all the disciplines that deal with food and drink, and a training center for many professions in the food industry.

The University of Pollenzo and Colorno must include teaching and research objectives, from the history of gastronomy to that of food technologies, and must also embrace geography, law, economics, marketing, sociology, anthropology, ecology, history of landscape, audiovisual communication, and tasting techniques. Overall, it must encompass a broad spectrum of interests and subjects, some of them innovative, capable of training gastronomes with the ability to work in journalism, the restaurant business, food marketing, the consortia that monitor the standards of different products, tourism, and the training and education sector. It represents the highest point yet reached in the educational strategy of Slow Food, and it will be an undertaking of international importance. An advisory committee will soon be set up to carry out a feasibility study for a second degree course on international eco-agriculture.

Chapter 4

The Noah Principle

Scenes from a Flood

On December 2, 1996, during the first Salone del Gusto held at
Turin's Lingotto Exhibition Center, Slow Food promoted a meeting to
discuss "Un'Arca del Gusto per salvare il pianeta dei sapori" (An Ark
of Taste to save the planet of flavors). Scholars of gastronomy, sociologists, political scientists, and gourmets were confronted with a
harsh fact: the worrying disappearance of competent craftspeople
and the systematic disappearance of fruit and vegetable species, of
products that are part of our folk memory, under the impact of disastrous agricultural policies that don't respect natural biorhythms,
the threat of environmental degradation, and hygiene laws drafted
for large industries that are absurd when applied to small artisan
producers. Faced with this situation, Slow Food set out a concrete
proposal with a symbolic name, the Ark, because an ark is what we
need to save quality food production from the flood of standardiza-

tion and its blighting effects. Faced with the logic of macroeconomics, we propose to go back to working on a regional scale and to invent new channels of production and supply, knowing that this is perhaps the only way to safeguard quality without losing sight entirely of European and world agriculture.

The very concept and symbol of the Ark carried with it a risk of misunderstanding, and (inevitably) the accusation that we were just a new incarnation of the conservative spirit. By emphasizing small-scale artisanal production and entrepreneurial capacity that respects the environment while ignoring the large-scale food industry that does, after all, exist, we ran the risk of shutting ourselves out of a very complex dynamic, and shutting ourselves up inside a snail shell. The fact is, none of us believed in the "good old days of yore," but everything seemed to indicate that our best game plan was to play defensively, because when the flood is at the gates, the only safe place is the Ark.

It was a book by a French sociologist, Michel Lacroix,[1] that convinced us we were right and showed us that to reaffirm "The Noah Principle" is not a rearguard action but an avant-garde response to the minefield of modernity that we have to traverse. After two centuries in which mankind has done everything possible to make itself master of the world, Lacroix maintains, at the dawn of the third millennium the myth of Prometheus no longer corresponds to the aspirations of contemporary man, and it is time to turn to a different model, the model of Noah. Faced with the excesses of modernization, we are not trying to change the world anymore, just to save it. Whether we are talking about the environment or the artistic heritage or the institutions of civil society, or—what we think is just as important—the great patrimony of knowledge attached to material culture, it is time to realize how fragile the world is and start to protect it, by creating a sanctuary for all that civilization has produced in the course of millennia and building a more human and highly developed society.

The progressive contraction of biodiversity, of the whole complex of natural environments and living species of animals and plants that populate our planet, is one of the most alarming aspects of the new millennium. In the last hundred years, 300,000 plant varieties have vanished from the earth, and the process is continuing at the rate of one variety every six hours. Every year 17 million hectares of forest disappear; since the beginning of the twentieth century we have lost 75 percent of the genetic diversity of our agricultural products, and today fewer than 30 plants nourish 95 percent of the world population. The agricultural industry is compromising the equilibrium of the ecosystem by wiping out traditional varieties and favoring the spread of monocultures with high yields, but high vulnerability. Telling examples of this include the corn blight that destroyed corn to the value of $1 billion in the United States in the 1970s, and the contemporary spread of the rickets virus that devastated the rice fields of Indonesia. In both cases, the only thing that saved vital forms of agriculture from disaster was the availability of older indigenous varieties.

The situation of domesticated animals is just as bad. In Europe half the breeds that existed at the beginning of the twentieth century have disappeared, and a third of those that remain risk following them into oblivion in the next twenty years. Losing a breed means giving up a unique and unrepeatable genetic heritage, the result of thousands of years of selection by man and by nature, forever, yet modern livestock operations are based on a handful of breeds chosen for the intensive production of meat, milk, and eggs. Preserving biodiversity, though, is vital for the future of the planet: evolution, the mechanism that allows life to adapt itself to environmental change, is impossible without a rich reservoir of ecosystems, breeds, and regional varieties.

Italy, with the extraordinary heritage of its geographic, climatic, and environmental variety, is an emblematic case: a rich country with great potential where agriculture continues to marginalize and abandon traditional crops, to the point where 1,500 varieties of fruit are at risk, while 80 percent of the apples produced belong to just four cultivars (botanical varieties). Out of a huge patrimony of vegetables, many varieties now survive almost exclusively in family gardens, and the fate of a great many breeds of domesticated animals appears to be sealed.

The disappearance of an animal breed or a plant variety forces us to renounce the flavors of a particular territory, of certain kinds of meat (fresh or cured) or cheese, for example; when indigenous breeds are replaced by other, more productive ones, there is, always and inevitably, a change in our sensory experience of food. The new version of the product we were used to is usually more banal, and it can even happen that a new raw material cannot be made into a foodstuff in the traditional way, so that along with the old breed, we lose the old product. On the other hand, a breed can sometimes be saved by raising the profile of the product, as happened with Reggiana cows, bovines typically raised in the flatlands of northern Italy, which were saved by the successful marketing of Parmigiano Reggiano cheese, which gets its special flavor from the special milk those cows give. This is an exemplary, but unfortunately an isolated, case, as local and traditional products continue to disappear one after the other. Barely seven years elapsed between the 1993 edition of the *Atlante dei prodotti tipici* (Atlas of products specific to individual territories) published by the National Institute of Rural Sociology, and the publication by Slow Food in 1999 of *Formaggi d'Italia* (Italian cheeses), and there are at least 100 kinds of cheese that are no longer present and accounted for: inimitable products like Granone from Lodi, Solandro from the Trentino region, Padraccio from the Basilicata region, and many others. In the space of a generation, every single one of the traditional varieties could be wiped out by competition from industrial cheeses free of blemishes and completely nondescript, like the mozzarella from pasteurized cow's milk that always tastes the same and is just as easy to make in Singapore as in Philadelphia or Oslo.

The flood of standardization doesn't just affect cheese and cured meat. It threatens to overwhelm all the artisanal food production of Italy and Europe, including bread, herbal products, wine, and vegetable oils. In 1992 the European Community (now the European Union) created the "PDO" (*Denominazione di origine protetta* or "Protected designation of origin") and the "PGI" (*Indicazione geografica protetta* or "Protected geographical indication") in order to help defend specialized local products, and they are important steps, but inadequate to protect our agro-alimentary heritage. The "PDO" identifies a product that is grown or raised, and processed, within a well-defined geographical area, while to obtain PGI status, it is enough if just one of the phases of production takes place in the area in question. To be awarded one of these designations, a production code, a guarantee from an outside agency, and approval from the EU are all required. Obviously small-scale producers with few resources will fail to clear these hurdles. It is indeed true that the institution of the PDO and the PGI have helped to combat fraud, but a production code is always the first step toward standardization, for all producers tend to adjust their particular styles to the strictures of the code, with the consequent loss of a whole gamut of small variations in flavor and texture. The PDO may guarantee that a product is what it claims to be, but does nothing to enhance its value otherwise. And it often seems as though, in the EU, the distribution of PDO and PGI designations is like any other bureaucratic and political process, and has nothing to do with the effective quality of the products designated.

That is not all, for the food and agriculture policies of the EU are tremendously contradictory. On one hand they establish programs to heighten the appreciation of local specialties and develop marginal agricultural areas, while on the other they continue to promulgate laws and regulations that slash at the very roots of the local individuality, the quality, and thus the future of many representative products like bread (bread makers are free to put any food substance at all into the dough), pasta (which can even be made without hard wheat flour), meat (the permitted quantity of dioxin has been doubled), and chocolate (vegetable fat can be substituted for cocoa butter).

Yet there are signs of renewed interest in specialized local production. Europe has realized that its alimentary heritage is too rich and varied to be forced into the straitjacket of the current hygiene standards, and so has mandated that member states may apply specific regulations to specific situations. But the bureaucratic procedure is lengthy, and in the meantime numerous small-scale, high-quality producers need immediate concrete help in order to survive.

Overall, the panorama is alarming: biodiversity in crisis, animal breeds and plant varieties facing extinction, kinds of cheese and cured meat lost forever, and the tools to protect them either ill-suited or inadequate to the task. All this has driven Slow Food to take action to construct an Ark of Taste in order to preserve an extraordinary economic, social, and cultural heritage of peasant and artisan traditions, unwritten but rich and complex, and ancient skills and techniques. It is a treasury of cured meats, cheeses, cereals, vegetables, fruits, and local breeds that often owe their particularity and their exceptional flavor to their isolation and their forced adaptation to difficult conditions.

The Ark and the Presidia

On June 29, 1997 Slow Food published the *Manifesto dell'Arca*:

To protect the small purveyors of fine food from the deluge of industrial standardization; to ensure the survival of endangered animal breeds, cheeses, cold cuts, edible herbs—both wild and cultivated—cereals, and fruit; to promulgate taste education; to make a stand against obsessive worrying about hygienic matters, which kills the specific character of many kinds of production; to protect the right to pleasure.

Leading figures from the worlds of culture, wine and food, scientific research, journalism, politics, and governmental institutions are endorsing a project articulated on two levels, scientific and popular. On one level, we have defined methods and research criteria, undertaken ethnobotanical, zoological, and historical research; trained experts in the field; and set up a documentation center. On the second, we have compiled and circulated a list of products at risk; analyzed them; disseminated knowledge about them and put them back into commercial circulation; promoted their adoption by restaurateurs; and tried to commit the government to preservation.

A scientific committee formed in January 1999 sets the selection criteria for the products that Slow Food intends to bring on board the Ark. There are five indispensable requirements: 1) they must be of excellent quality; 2) they must be species, varieties, plant ecotypes, and animal populations either indigenous or long adapted to a specific territory, or else made with local ingredients, and prepared and aged following traditional local practices; 3) they must be linked, environmentally, socioeconomically, and historically, to a specific area; 4) they must be made in limited quantities in firms of small size; 5) they must be at risk of extinction, real or potential.

The Ark of Taste is not meant to be a museum, nor does it claim to be able to save the genetic resources of the whole world, but it concentrates on that portion of the biosphere that arrives on our tables.

The aim is not to create experimental compounds, assemble animal and vegetable rarities, or serve hard-to-find and astronomically priced cheeses and cured meats at exclusive dinners. The Ark is a place for products with commercial potential, for which consumers will pay premium prices because of their superior flavor. Rather than use the worn-out word *tipici* ("typical" of a specific place, the equivalent of "old-fashioned" or "homemade" in English), we prefer to call these products "historical and localized." With the help of committed Slow Food Convivia, we will carry out a broad census of small-scale, high-quality food products from all five continents, in the belief that, just like the landscape, art, and the historical record, these things represent a heritage of humanity to be kept safe and to be appreciated.

The question, long debated, is what concrete steps to take to oppose the erosion of biodiversity, put a stop to agro-alimentary standardization, and avoid the progressive disappearance of things produced in small quantities. Theoretically speaking, the terms of the problem are clear enough. Since the Ark project was launched at the Salone del Gusto at Turin in 1996, a lot of detailed work and research have been carried out. The scientific committee has listed and catalogued around 450 Italian products that meet the specifications: local origin, tradition, restricted quantities, and gastronomic excellence. Our members know what these things mean, and so do the restaurateurs, businesspeople, and wine producers who keep an eye on what Slow Food is up to. Even the governmental institutions, after years of disastrous agricultural policies aimed at increasing production and rationalizing the cultivated part of the country's land surface, are beginning to see the light. Concepts like locally specific products, eco-compatible agriculture, intensity of flavor, and traditional techniques are being heard about more and more often in the media as well, even in popular television programming. But while this wave of communication is rising, the products themselves continue to disappear, or else hang on by their fingernails in a desperate situation of increasing marginalization and insufficient economic reward. So was born the idea, risky but fascinating, of going directly to the land and taking action.

It is a dramatic role change. Slow Food has always refrained from being a direct player in the economy, drawing its effectiveness and credibility from its character as a cultural and recreational association. But at the assembly of the fiduciaries at Bologna in November 1999, a new strategy was approved, and the project of the Presidia was born. Actually the word "Presidium," which literally means "garrison fortress," raised a few eyebrows at first, since it brings to mind trumpet fanfares and military salutes and seems to imply some sort of armed occupation. But it isn't easy to find another word that signifies the action of safeguarding and protecting as directly as "Presidium" does, and the Italian verb *presidiare* also bears the meanings "to protect" and "to reinforce." As people got used to the word, it caught on surprisingly fast, and although not everyone likes it, it perfectly conveys the intended notion.

The problems are mostly in the existing situation. As everyone knows, Italy is one of the countries with the largest number of local food specialties in the world. But this galaxy of generally middle-aged, or elderly, producers, fragmented, marginal, mistrustful, and fearful of a tidal wave of legislation and hygienic and sanitary regulation, is not a coherent system, or one that will be easy to rationalize. Every product presents its own proper specificity and problems. Intervening directly might mean something quite different from one case to another. Here are some examples.

Every year around 1,300,000 rounds of PDO Asiago cheese are produced. So what we have is a locally specific product produced in large quantities. Yet even here a Presidium is fundamentally important, for not many people realize that there is an especially good kind that is produced in small quantities: Asiago Stravecchio, a cheese produced only from milk obtained during summer pasturing in the mountains and aged for at least 18 months. The job of the Presidium is to distinguish and raise the profile of these rounds (10,000 at most), and make consumers aware of the extraordinary flavor profile of Asiago Stravecchio. Further, it must also convince the herders to continue to spend their summers in their alpine huts; preserve the traditional breed of cattle, the Rendena; and age the cheese properly instead of selling it when young to the dealers. All without devaluing normal Asiago, which is itself a noble traditional cheese: a tricky operation.

Ventricina del Vastese is a traditional cured meat from the Abruzzi that illustrates another kind of problem. Every farmstead, practically every family, uses the best parts of their own home-grown pigs and cures them slowly, to produce a cured raw meat spherical in form. It could be an important economic resource for the area, but every bit of it produced is grabbed up immediately: the few Ventricine not consumed directly by the producers are sold to neighbors or to emigrants from the district who return home during the summer holidays, and the prices are astronomical, probably higher than the market would accept. In this case, to raise the profile of the product would be useless, if not deleterious. What the Presidium has to do is convince the producers to raise more pigs organically and sell more Ventricine into the market, at a more affordable price.

There are other cases as well, just as tricky, in which traditional techniques cannot be left completely unchanged. In Sardinia, for example, Casizolu, a spun-curd cheese made with the milk of Sardo-Modicana cattle, a native breed raised wild in the pasturelands of Montiferru, has the potential to bring economic development to the Montiferru area. But this extremely rare cheese is made following procedures that frequently undermine its quality of flavor. The task here is to convince those producers not simply to resign themselves to the often unpleasantly bitter flavor, not simply to accept small defects out of habit, but to improve their production methods, exchange information, compare their cheese with the great spun-curd cheeses of Italy, and build small cheese factories that are up to code. It takes a lot of work to make contact with them and persuade them that their cheese could be a valuable commodity, for ancient mistrust and longstanding isolation have to be overcome. Five families have accepted Slow Food's invitation, giving proof of their capacity to widen their mental horizons, observing and tasting, listening to and heeding criticism, showing that they are prepared to try out new techniques in order to correct the imperfections arising from a tradition of making cheese exclusively for home consumption. A production discipline has been drafted that lays down precise norms regarding the raw material and methods of production and preservation, in order to guarantee reliable high quality. The selection of the milk to be used is one of the most important points: the only kind allowed is from Sardo-Modicana cows. These families have structured themselves as small businesses, with workplaces that are up to code, and have taken a training course given by a technician from the animal husbandry department of the University of Sassari.

The tactic adopted in the case of the Cinque Terre (Five Towns) area of Liguria is different yet again, and even more complex, for here the main concern was to safeguard the territory: the famous terracelike rock shelves where vines were once grown and that are now being progressively abandoned. In order to save the landscape, it was necessary to raise the quality of the Sciacchetrà wine produced on those terraces so that it could fetch a price high enough to make it worthwhile for some young people to take up vine cultivation there once more. The Presidium for the Cinque Terre worked in two directions, appealing for portions of the terrain to be adopted and promoting a sort of training course for young wine makers. The goal is to produce an adequate quantity of excellent Sciacchetrà, a sweet wine capable of rivaling the quality and price of the finest and costliest Sauternes of France.

As this handful of examples reveals, a Presidium needs to be agile, able to offer help and encouragement in many different situations. Slow Food's strength lies in the fact that it can count on a capillary network of informants in the localities, capable of dealing with organizations and official agencies and fully informed about products and businesses. Thanks mainly to this adaptability and its local roots, Slow Food was able to announce the creation of no fewer than 91 Presidia at the Salone del Gusto at Turin in October 2000. Obviously not all of them are fully up and running. Some are just getting started, but others have been active for years, like the one for Piedmontese meat; or robiola di Roccaverano, a goat's milk cheese from the Langa Astigiana; the Tuscan zolfino bean; and cicerchia, a rare type of chickpea from the Marche. All were started by particularly alert and enterprising "slowmen" and slow-women" on a volunteer basis, and are now high-profile "institutional" media platforms.

The Presidia project is ambitious and highly innovative. Admittedly there were some cases in which institutions and experts with a local presence, like agricultural associations and local governments, were already trying to relaunch products and crops at risk of extinction and preserve livestock breeds and techniques of cultivation. But their efforts mostly had low visibility, since they lacked connections and supporters. Slow Food has given them the boost they needed, providing them with a media spotlight and putting them in touch with the world of consumers and distributors, and above all linking them with one another. With the Salone del Gusto as the showroom, products from the Presidia have emerged into the open. All the producers, without exception, quickly sold out their stocks, and what is even more important, they laid the foundations at Turin for a future market composed of Slow Food members (the association has, in a few cases, taken a direct marketing role), alert and responsive wine bar and restaurant operators, and alternative channels of distribution, like e-commerce.

The Presidia will be, and in part already are, a system or network. And the more projects are launched, the more this network will be in a position to lay down new guidelines for other farmers and producers. In sum, this is a big wager, bringing together ancient and marginal professions and a new class of consumers disposed to pay a fair price in exchange for quality and outstanding flavor, and sensitive to the need to protect the environment and the food supply. The strategy moves, and has to move, from the bottom up, since the Eurobureaucrats in Brussels look askance at local specialty products. Hence we don't expect much help from the EU; quite the contrary. Public opinion in some EU countries is hostile to GMOs and firmly opposed to the wasteful EU policy of overproduction and stockpiling (the wine lakes and butter mountains). So we have to act fast.

Slow Food's aim is to export the idea of the Presidia to other countries, although one thing has to be kept in mind: in France 80 percent of the people, and in Italy 75 percent, know what local specialty products are (the data are from Eurobarometro), but in Sweden, for example, the statistics show that barely 8 percent of consumers are that well informed. Outside the Mediterranean basin, it may be necessary to place more emphasis on landscape preservation and organic production than on traditional foods. But the "new agriculture" we want also means fields free of pesticides, healthy and nontransgenic crops, foods with distinctive flavors, and farmers earning enough to live civilly and happily.

In the Third World, the policy of creating Presidia will be strategically important. In the past, Slow Food experimented with the so-called *Tavole Fraterne*, Fraternal Tables, collections of funds to be spent on projects for upgrading and development, or in the case of the Yanomani Indians of Amazonia, on hospitals; in all cases, the purpose is to ensure the preservation of traditional foods and the traditions and the customs of given areas. It hasn't escaped us, though, that these kinds of intervention, despite their originality, do not differ much from normal charitable giving, inspired by Eurocentric ideas and lacking focus on development. Charity, no matter how useful, is something Slow Food rejects because it doesn't respect the cultural elements of populations and tends to see them as entities needing "salvation," and therefore "conquest."

With this strongly held belief, what we want to do is extend our associational structure and our work to the less wealthy areas of the planet, in adaptive and sustainable forms. Respect for cultural diversity, and the knowledge that people cannot be saved unless they are enabled to understand the world and grasp that they too possess material riches, is the primary conviction of Slow Food. The difference is well summed up in the classic fishing metaphor: it is more useful to teach someone how to fish than to give him fish. The goal of future Slow Food Presidia in the underdeveloped areas will be to recuperate and make known traditional knowledges, so that they become motors of development and prosperity. Let it be clear: the "poor" countries are actually rich, with an extraordinary patrimony of plant and animal species, ancient local cultures, and untapped human potential. Defending and promoting them from below, on the basis of individual and collective differences, can make it possible to start a process of intellectual and material growth that will profit the whole world. The western model, imposed from above, should be left behind. No one can impose a standardizing model on the treasure chest of (bio)diversity that is our planet. More than 130 Italian and 19 international Presidia are currently active.

Quality, the Law, and Biotech

Ideally, the laws would be framed as instruments to protect the quality of goods, but the concept of quality is, in itself, an abstraction. What is the idea of quality at which legislation aims? Essentially it is seen as a question of health protection, when not as a purely industrial matter. In 1999 the European Union promulgated the set of norms known as HACCP (Hazard Analysis Critical Control Point), and it was immediately obvious that their sole purpose was to make prohibitions and requirements uniform, and products safe through sterilization. Cheese that has been aged underground in a *fossa* (pit), as is the tradition in Romagna, will not pass the test of HACCP because it contains molds and bacteria, which, although they give it its specific taste and its "handcrafted quality," draw the fire of the snipers of health science because they see them as health risks. That and other kinds of cheese like Roquefort, or the cured meat known as Culatello that is aged for months in grottos and cellars rich in bacterial flora, cannot be guaranteed to suit places with gleaming tiles, or the legislative logic that sees big industries—what a contradiction!—as the only possible guarantors of a product's safety. That is not the theoretical road that Slow Food is following (and has shown to be feasible through the strategy of the Ark and the Presidia) toward a healthy agriculture producing local specialties, an agriculture that is not a noose for producers and doesn't impoverish odors and flavors that are the sediment of centuries of experience; an agriculture not standardized for consumers.

Yet the law is something we can't do without in an epoch like this, with science subservient to agribusiness, precisely because it is the law that will have to regulate and safeguard the health of consumers in the delicate matter of GMOs, in which Slow Food is following a prudent and cautious line from the health point of view and outright resistance from the quality point of view. We have touched on the matter in previous chapters, and now it is time to focus on some of the aspects that cause us the most disquiet. All I shall do is set forth a few facts, letting readers draw the conclusions they see fit.

First, a bit of history. June 1980 was a crucial date, for at that time a judgment of the United States Supreme Court recognized the legitimacy of an invention of Ananda Mohan Chakrabarty, the first to patent a genetically modified bacterium and open the doors to unimaginable, yet suddenly hugely attractive, profit opportunities for the multinationals of genetic manipulation.

Since that date, there has been a mad race to adulterate DNA. In 1982 the first transgenic animals and mutant-gene strawberries, into which the gene of a northern fish species was injected to make them more cold-resistant, were created. In 1983 transgenic plants were created, and in 1986 they were put on the market. In 1994 the Methusalem tomato, which doesn't go bad for months, even after being picked, appeared; and then, in an aberrant climax of manipulation, we had beetroots with artichoke genes, antiviral zucchini, piglets with accelerated fertility, bees without stings, frogs without heads, and today, all around us, potatoes, corn, and soybeans genetically modified to resist the pesticides sold by the very same multinationals. Transgenic plants are now cultivated on 40 million hectares of the planet, almost 75 percent of them in the United States.

Now let's review some of the reasons for holding back—or if you prefer, list a few ideas to stimulate discussion:

1. The biotechnologies applied to agriculture are at present entirely under the control of the multinationals, the only entities capable of funding the research. GMOs have been put onto the market, especially soy and corn, in a deceptive manner and with no information supplied to consumers, who have discovered that they

were already consuming these organisms without knowing it. GMOs may be forbidden in Europe, but Italy imports soybeans and corn from the United States in the form of animal feed products and lecithin from soybeans, which is regularly found in mayonnaise, biscuits, and many other industrially produced foodstuffs.

2. The laboratory tests that guarantee the harmlessness of GMOs are tainted by a temporal imbalance that ought to put us on our guard: since these are not new varieties but new species, ecosystems that have been tested in millions of years of evolution cannot be suddenly altered on the basis of "reassuring" tests lasting a few years. Never in world history has man inserted new species into nature, and the consequences, as things stand, are unforeseeable in the long run. Nor is the insertion limited to some marginal corner of the world, although that would be serious enough. What is going on is a profound mutation of agriculture over vast areas of the planet, which are being carpeted with transgenic crops.

3. Multinationals like Monsanto and Novartis sell transgenic soy plants that automatically produce toxins able to defeat parasites. This has led to the appearance of new parasite species, more resistant organisms able to breach the immune defenses of transgenic plants, and history has already taught us that the strategy of strengthening herbicides (think of DDT) leads to the evolution of viruses and parasites that, in time, adapt to the changed conditions, with grave risk to neighboring ecosystems. Nor do these toxins break down into the environment: they remain in the part of the plants that is not used and the fields where they are grown. The quantity is more than what would be required to defeat the parasites if modern combined systems were used to protect the crops (crop monitoring and targeted intervention when the danger point is reached, in the areas attacked by that specific parasite). So the justification often put forward by these same multinationals,

that transgenics reduces the quantity of artificial plant treatment products put into circulation, does not hold water.

4. A hard barrier between transgenic crops and nontransgenic ones, when growing takes place in the open, is not feasible, inasmuch as pollen, bacteria, and insects do not respect property boundaries. A transgenic field develops and favors more resistant parasites, which, if they do not thrive in the GMO crop itself, have only to move into the adjacent, defenseless field and spread from there, in ways and with results that nobody yet knows.

5. A field on which GMOs have been grown cannot be returned to traditional crops. The soil is infected for over 30 years, and there is a risk of contributing to the process of desertification that is already advancing at an exponential rate. The idea underlying transgenic agriculture is hyperproduction, requiring high dosages of fertilizer and high levels of irrigation, unsustainable on a planet on which water will become one of the most serious problems of the coming years.

6. GMOs are a grave threat to biodiversity. Every six hours a plant species becomes extinct somewhere in the world, and a report from the Food and Agricultural Organization of the United Nations in 1991 forecasts that within a few years the same fate will befall 30 percent of the breeds of domesticated animals that still exist. Think about this: in the Neolithic, humans consumed more than 5,000 plant varieties spontaneously; today their alimentation is restricted to 150 varieties (of which only 30 or so are eaten in large amounts), and that number is destined to shrink in coming decades. In the demented drive toward a world of tomatoes that don't go bad and strawberries with salmon genes, indigenous species and varieties selected by tradition, their flavors, and the opportunity (of which we have already availed ourselves in the past) of finding varieties resistant to the attack of

certain parasites in the far corners of the earth are all being sacrificed. As well as the recent cases of American corn and Indonesian rice, the example of the potato is enlightening. After the dearth of the mid-nineteenth century, when all the European potato crops were attacked by the Phytophthora fungus, recovery was made possible by resorting to a variety found in Peru. The same principle applies in the case of Phylloxera, from which recovery was made possible by planting vines from American stock. Now, on the contrary, try to imagine all the crops in the world converted to the same transgenic species. When highly resistant parasites develop, where will we find the alternative varieties we need to survive?

7. A problem with serious implications is patent laws. At present the traditional varieties and species are the patrimony of humanity, and are available to all. Transgenic species, however, become the property of just one firm through the acquisition of a patent. With the massive conversion to transgenics that is occurring, we all risk becoming economically dependent on a few multinationals, which, by commercializing sterile GMOs, force farmers to buy seeds from them every year. This is the most violent agricultural revolution that has ever occurred. Farmers now do no more than carry out orders that arrive from on high, and lose any bond to the earth they cultivate. Once it was farmers themselves who selected and perpetuated seeds, but with transgenics, they are forced to purchase them. Imagine the degree of economic and social dependence that results.

8. Another mystification surrounding the *dei ex machina* we call GMOs is the claim that these crops help to overcome hunger in the world. We do an injustice to the complexity of the problem if we treat "hunger" as a problem of production and ignore the opposing logic that inspires world agriculture. Through production subsidies we have actually favored excess production, which

still doesn't go to feed the world's hungry because of problems of distribution. It is money, always and solely, or the lack of it, that keeps the regime of exploitation and underdevelopment going. Here it is enough to note the recent polemics about GMO grapes: if transgenics were developed to battle hunger, why spend time and money on research on wine grapes—i.e., on a consumer product that, from a worldwide perspective, is a luxury item?

In light of all this, we have only the law to rely on to protect us from the invisible presence of GMO products in our food. Slow Food hopes that experiments of this kind are taken out of the hands of the multinationals, and that information about them is guaranteed by impartial bodies that take the job of watching over research seriously. It is almost utopian to hope for this, given that science has never bothered to account, or ask permission, for its experiments. Complete and accurate labeling is the consumer's last line of defense at this point. The laws currently on the books are insufficient. Let's take the case of transgenic lecithin again. Because it derives from transgenic soybeans but does not contain the modified portion of DNA, it has the same status as the kind derived from non-GMO plants when it comes to labeling. This is misleading information, which Slow Food wishes to see supplanted by much more complete labeling. We think that consumers have the right not to be deceived about foodstuffs, especially in an age when assorted scandals have taught them to read the label carefully and made them quite rightly fearful about what they eat. Legal sleight of hand to flout the truth, and not just when it comes to transgenics, is a bad and persistent habit that favors deceit of the palate and profit for those who commit it.

One last point, anything but comforting, concerns a gap that has plagued the labeling of the foods that wind up on our tables for years. When you see the word "flavorings" on the package, don't imagine that it always refers to natural substances, or at the limit, even harmless ones. This word, and words like it, are a cloak to conceal otherwise undeclared chemical aromatizers, preservatives, colorants, and flavor enhancers (the list goes on and on) used to make products of poor quality appetizing. The experiment that would prove this is hard to make, but if you could taste a cured meat, a brioche, a breakfast cereal, a drink, or any other industrial product that had not been flavor- or color-enhanced with these magic "flavorings," you would probably find that it was something you would not have been tempted to buy in the first place, and that the flavor was a disappointment.

The Slow Food Award for the Defense of Biodiversity

When our projects for the Ark and the Presidia had been launched, our knowledge that an invisible army of humanity was working to safeguard species and products in the name of biodiversity gave us a fresh idea: a prize to be awarded to people who had made significant contributions to that struggle.

The resulting initiative, the Slow Food Award for the Defense of Biodiversity, is now in its third year. So far it has been staged in Bologna, Italy (2000), Oporto, Portugal (2001), and Turin, Italy (2002). It works as follows. Through a jury of journalists, experts, scholars, and aficionados from around the world, Slow Food receives information about people who merit this kind of recognition. Proposals arrive from every continent to recognize people who are advancing our struggle simply by working at trades that have been revived, or jealously protected, or invented, and that create and spread cultural knowledge of great worth. Slow Food wants to bring these men and women to international attention, make their stories known, gratify them, and at the same time help them to keep up the fight and persevere on the path they have chosen. The prize consists of a sum of money, and is given annually to 13 chosen individuals. From among these, the jury, which holds a meeting at the time of the event, chooses five to receive a special prize, awarded in the media spotlight to give them even greater prominence.

The spectacle of an audience of 500 jury members who come together from every corner of the planet at the behest of Slow Food, and the 13 bewildered prizewinners, leaves an indelible image in the memory of those present and those who have labored toward this initiative. What Slow Food is becoming is palpable here: a melting pot of diverse and very different cultures, brought together by a common purpose. The varied styles of dress, the array of facial features and skin colors that have come together to pay homage to those 13 small heroes, leave their mark. The international dimension is truly global in this case, because differences become a form of wealth, and variety a tangible value.

The kinds of work chosen are many, and the tie that binds them is subtle yet strong. The winners include people like Jesus Garzón, a Spaniard who has dedicated his life to reviving an ancient agricultural practice, transhumance herding, in a country that has lived through rapid industrial development in recent years. This was once a noble occupation in Spain, where shepherds were given many privileges in support of a hard and lonely style of life, but it lost much of its allure with the advent of industrialization, and the upshot of its gradual decline has been grave damage to the ecosystem. He fully understood the value of transhumance in the context of the recovery of biodiversity in Spain, and took up this occupation with no financial support. Since 1992 others have joined him in Spain, and the advantageous results have been observed: the growth of wild grass is better controlled, reducing the risk of fire along the routes used; plant species are efficiently spread because their seeds become lodged in the coats of the sheep, and are thus carried far and wide; the forests are cleared of undergrowth, favoring repopulation by species from small birds to wolves; handcrafted sheep's milk cheeses are increasingly prized; and the native breeds of sheep dogs are being saved from extinction. This is true conservatism, refurbishing ancient professions and knowledges, and the objection might be raised that it amounts to the nostalgic refusal of, perhaps even a hindrance to, modern development in a nation like Spain. Actually it is an important choice, on account of its cultural value, its social value (popular festivals take place when the shepherds pass through), its economic value (many unemployed young men, sons of shepherds, have returned to their fathers' profession with satisfaction and pride), and its ecological value.

A different case is that of entrepreneurial ventures in underdeveloped areas, which creatively exploit the scant local resources to improve the community's quality of life. While respecting usage and custom, they do not hold development back; indeed, they give it incentive, in ways that fit in with the nature of the place. Take the idea of Nancy Jones: to set up a dairy operation in Mauritania in order to commercialize milk from camels, goats, and cows, and cheeses made from them. This initiative has not only brought jobs, development, and prosperity, it has stimulated the consumption of products obtained from camel's milk, which the nomadic shepherds of the Mauritanian desert had always regarded as taboo. With this taboo erased, the trade has developed, allowing the nomads to continue to lead the life they prefer, without disturbing the natural equilibrium of the desert in which they live. The prize went to Nancy Jones because she showed how new impetus can be given to Third World communities without violating them. She has improved the lives of the nomads, and the award given her is for her perseverance, because she goes out to get the camel's milk herself instead of having it brought to the dairy, making the effort to track down the tribes in the desert and thus allowing them to maintain their traditions and habits unchanged.

Another example of work in impoverished parts of the world is that of Raúl Antonio Manuel, the young leader of the indigenous community of Rancho Grande, in the mountains of the state of Oaxaca in Mexico. Here we have a model of cooperative production and social organization applied in a village in the region of Chinantla, rough country and hard to traverse, where the main products are coffee and vanilla. The inhabitants speak different dialects and knowledge of Spanish is limited. Cultural identity is strongly felt, and has been reinforced in recent years by the guerrilla movement against the government and for the Indians in Chiapas. In Chinantla a large-scale effort is under way to "fix" the indigenous culture by giving the native languages written form for the first time using the Roman alphabet, and teaching them in the schools.

The initiative of Raúl Antonio Manuel is part of this context of resistance by the local cultures. Rancho Grande is a small community of 200 people that has been able to create its own regulations governing agricultural production, social behavior, and environmental protection, and live by them. All this came about because of a simple but decisive idea of Raúl's: to compete with the large coffee growers by going for quality. The first step was to select the seeds to be used throughout the area, so that the labeling of the product as a local specialty would really mean something. Then production techniques were improved, by acquiring machinery for the community and stressing cleanness and the recycling of the water used in the process. In this way the quality of the product was raised and the environmental impact reduced. Moreover, knowing the risk arising from fluctuations in the price of coffee, the community decided to develop another source of income, vanilla. With the help of a group of university researchers, they succeeded in reviving a form of cultivation that was dying out, reacquainting the peasant farmers with things that they had forgotten themselves. This corner of the world is sending a clear message about rural development to all of us.

These three stories show how the purpose of Slow Food is to encourage those, in rich areas and in poor, who are working, out of the limelight and mostly with no help from local governments, *against* the economic logic of modern life but *in* this "modern" world. They are examples of human ingenuity and of how it is possible to work in harmony with nature; these events and lives represent a new paradigm.

The example of Jesus Garzón is emblematic of the project that Slow Food proposes in the more developed parts of the world. Marked by a pragmatism typical of the association, his work indicates a viable route for the conversion to a new agriculture, one more respectful of natural and socioeconomic equilibria and compatible with an industrial or postindustrial society. By reviving a centuries-old tradition and bringing an occupation up to date—the shepherds take turns, are equipped with cellular phones, and receive visitors when they are lodging in the cabins that have been built for them and equipped with all the comforts—he has shown how the revitalization of an apparently outmoded agricultural sector may be of great benefit for the conservation of species and the improvement of the quality of life for all. The initiatives of Nancy Jones and Raúl Antonio Manuel, on the other hand, indicate what sorts of policy Slow Food should embrace for the Third World.

The award and the Presidia are study projects, practical undertakings, and above all, the backbone of an association that makes work, information, and the international spirit its guidelines. The gastronome, if that means a passive beneficiary of agricultural resources and the wealth they generate, is yesterday's man, his ethic of profit and enjoyment compromised by the very world that legitimates him.

Lacking a sense of responsibility toward both our alimentary heritage and its future users, and an awareness of the ethical choices that this heritage imposes, he has no future. Today the paradox of pleasure is the discipline you have to impose on yourself in pursuit of it, and the variety of forms that it can assume. For much of the nineteenth and twentieth centuries, excellence when it came to taste meant the hegemony of a single culinary model in commerce and production, exemplified concretely in French haute cuisine. The decline of imperialism in taste, or rather its revival in the seemingly more democratic form of fast food, made an effort to bring new roles and strategies into being imperative, along with the acceptance of diversity as the principle of unified action for quality in food.

In a world that appears ineluctably condemned to the standardization of all products and the flattening out of all flavors, a world whose resources have been harnessed to the interests and profits of a few, Slow Food sees its international vocation as a proposal for an alternative model of development. Concrete actions and feasible projects are more congenial to us than denial and protest. Every corner of the world is guarding a portion of biodiversity that is under threat every day from those who see man and nature merely as riches to be exploited. The first objective is to spread knowledge and enlarge awareness; starting from there, we can give dignity and economic life to every territory, embracing diversity as a thing of value and the techniques of globalization themselves as a vehicle for enhancing its value and making it known. The model of the Presidia, applied with success in Italy, can show us a road to follow everywhere in the world: putting a premium on, and building up, local resources, with their extraordinary variety, making local products known and appreciated throughout a community of attentive and sensitive consumers, means offering the world the hope of a future different from the polluted and tasteless one that the lords of the earth have programmed for all of us.

Without Nostalgia

I have chosen the essay form to record the many faces and phases of a movement that, from one year to the next, is never what it used to be, though it is growing all the time; a movement that speaks many languages as if they were only one. To the peasants of Rancho Grande, to the caravans of Mauritania, to our members scattered in every corner of the world, and to those who are reading about Slow Food here for the first time, I dedicate this book. In it I have included a little bit of history, individual and collective, and put on record ideas that were once no more than ideas and that have now become concrete facts. Above all, this book is about our own short-term future: without the Slow Food Award, the Ark, or the Presidia, taking pleasure in eating and conviviality would be mere nostalgia. That is the one sentiment I am unable to feel, and I wanted to make that clear by putting this dedication at the end of the book, in the knowledge that tomorrow I will have to repeat it again, probably, in different words.

For their valuable help, I wish to thank Alberto Capatti, Giovanni Ruffa, Alessandro Monchiero, and Carlo Bogliotti.

—C.P.

Appendices

The Slow Food Italian Presidia

VAL D'AOSTA

Toma di Gressoney—cow's-milk cheese

PIEDMONT

Agnello Sambucano—Sambucano lamb

Cappone di Morozzo—Morozzo capon

Cardo gobbo di Nizza Monferrato—Nizza Monferrato "hunchback" cardoon

Cevrin di Coazze—goat's-milk cheese

Coniglio Grigio di Carmagnola—Carmagnola gray rabbit

Filetto baciato di Ponzone—cured meat

Fragola di Tortona—Tortona strawberry

Gallina Bionda Piemontese/Gallina Bianca di Saluzzo—Piedmontese blonde hen/Saluzzo white hen

Maccagno—cow's-milk cheese

Montébore—cow's-milk cheese

Mortadella della Val d'Ossola—Val d'Ossola mortadella

Moscato passito della Valle Bagnario di Strevi—Moscato Passito wine of the Valle Bagnario di Strevi

Mustardela delle Valli Valdesi—blood sausage

Paste di meliga del Monregalese—Mondovì melic biscuits

Peperone corno di Bue di Carmagnola—Carmagnola "ox-horn" capsicum

Razza Piemontese—Piedmontese ox

Robiola di Roccaverano classica—goat's-milk cheese

Sarass del Fen—sheep's-milk/cow's-milk cheese

Testa in cassetta di Gavi—cured meat

Tinca gobba dorata del pianalto di Poirino—Poirino tench

Tuma di pecora delle Langhe—sheep's-milk cheese

Vecchie varietà di mele piemontesi—heirloom Piedmontese apple varieties

LOMBARDY

Bagòss di Bagolino—cow's-milk cheese

Grano saraceno della Valtellina—Valtellina buckwheat

Salame Mantovano—salami

Tombea—cow's-milk cheese

Violino di capra della Valchiavenna—cured goat meat

TRENTINO ALTO ADIGE

Casolèt—cow's-milk cheese

Ciuighe del Banale—cured meat

Lucanica trentina—salami

Mortandela della Val di Non—cured meat

Puzzone di Moena—cow's-milk cheese

Vezzena—cow's-milk cheese

Vino Santo Trentino—wine

VENETO

Agnello d'Alpago—Alpago lamb

Stravecchio di malga—cow's-milk cheese

Carciofo Violetto di Sant'Erasmo—Sant'Erasmo purple artichoke

Gallina padovana—Padovana hen

Mais Biancoperla—Biancoperla corn

Morlacco del Grappa—cow's-milk cheese

Riso di Grumolo delle Abbadesse—Grumolo delle Abbadesse rice

Vacca Burlina—Burlina cow

FRIULI VENEZIA GIULIA

Pitina, Petuccia, Peta—cured meats

LIGURIA

Acciughe di Monterosso—Monterosso anchovies

Aglio di Vessalico—Vessalico garlic

Aspargo Violetto d'Albenga—Albenga violet asparagus

Castagna essiccata nei tecci di Calizzano e Murialdo—dried Calizzano and Murialdo chestnuts

Cicciarelli di Noli—Noli anchovies

Fagioli di Badalucco, Conio e Pigna—Badalucco, Conio, and Pigna beans

Focaccia classica di Genova—classic Genoa focaccia

Sciacchetrà delle Cinque Terre—dessert wine

EMILIA-ROMAGNA

Anguilla marinata di Comacchio—marinated Comacchio eel

Culatello di Zibello—cured meat

Mariola—boiling sausage

Mortadella classica di Bologna—classic Bologna mortadella

Raviggiolo dell'Appennino tosco-romagnolo—cow's-milk/sheep's-milk/goat's-milk cheese

Razza bovina Romagnola—Romagnola cow

Razza suina Mora Romagnola—Mora Romagnola pig

Salama da Sugo—boiling sausage

Salmerino del Corno delle Scale—Corno alle Scale char

Spalla Cruda—raw ham

TUSCANY

Agnello di Zeri—Zeri lamb

Biroldo della Garfagnana—cured meat

Bottarga di Orbetello—Orbetello gray mullet roe

Chianina Classica—classic Chianina ox

Cinta Senese—pig breed

Cipolla di Certaldo—Certaldo onion

Cucina goym nelle città del tufo—Jewish confectionery of the Tuscan Maremma

Fagiolo di zolfino—Zolfino bean

Fico secco di Carmignano—Carmignano dried fig

Lardo di Colonnata—cured meat

Mallegato—cured meat

Marocca di Casola—Casola chestnut bread

Mortadella di Prato—Prato mortadella

Palamita dell'Arcipelago Toscano—Tuscan Island palamita (fish)

Pane di patate della Garfagnana—Garfagnana potato bread

Pecorino della Montagna pistoiese—Pistoia mountain pecorino

Pollo del Valdarno—Valdarno chicken

Prosciutto del Casentino—ham

Vacca Maremmana—Maremmana cow

UMBRIA

Fagiolina del lago Trasimeno—Lake Trasimeno bean

Cipolla di Cannara—Cannara onion

MARCHE

Cicerchia di Serra de'Conti—pulse

Lonzino di fico—fig cake

Mele Rosa dei Monti Sibillini—Monti Sibillini red apples

Oliva tenera Ascolana—Ascoli olive

Salame di Fabriano—salami

Pecorino dei Monti Sibillini—sheep's-milk cheese

Vino di Visciole—black cherry wine

LAZIO

Coppiette di maremmana—cured meat

Marzolina—goat's-milk/sheep's-milk/cow's-milk cheese

ABRUZZO

Mortadelle di Campotosto—cured meat

Pecorino di Farindola—sheep's-milk cheese

Ventricina del Vastese—cured meat

PUGLIA

Agrumi del Gargano—citrus fruits

Anguilla di Lesina—eel

Caciocavallo Podolico del Gargano—cow's milk

Capocollo di Martina Franca—cured meat

Fava di Carpino—Carpino broad bean

Pane Tradizionale di Altamura—traditional Altamura bread

CAMPANIA

Alici di Menaica—Menaica anchovies

Carciofo Violetto di Catellammare—Castellammare violet artichoke

Conciato Romano—cow's-milk/sheep's-milk/goat's-milk cheese

Coniglio da fossa di Ischia—Ischia cave rabbit

Gamberetto di nassa—Nassa shrimp

Limone Sfusato di Amalfi—Amalfi lemon

Mozzarella nella Mortella—mozzarella wrapped in myrtle leaves

Pomodorino al Piennolo—tomato variety

Pomodoro San Marzano—San Marzano tomatoes

Provolone del Monaco—cow's-milk cheese

Soppressata di Gioi—cured meat

BASILICATA

Casieddu di Moliterno—goat's-milk cheese

Caciocavallo Podolico della Basilicata—cow's-milk cheese

Melanzana di Rotonda—Rotonda eggplant

CALABRIA

Fico Dottato cosentino—Cosenza stuffed fig

Pecorino del Monte Poro—sheep's-milk cheese

SICILY

Aglio rosso di Nùbia—Nùbia red garlic

Asino Ragusano—Ragusano donkey

Bottarga di Favignana—Favignana tuna roe

Cappero di Salina e Pantelleria—Salina and Pantelleria caper

Capra Girgentana—Girgentana goat

Fava Larga di Leonforte—Leonforte broad bean

Lenticchia di Ustica—Ustica lentil

Maiorchino—sheep's-milk cheese

Mandorle di Noto—Noto almonds

Manna delle Madonie—Madonie manna

Meloni d'inverno—winter melons

Pane nero di Castelvetrano—Castelvetrano black bread

Pesche tardive di Leonforte—late-harvest Leonforte peaches

Pesche Tabacchiere dell'Etna—Etna "snuffbox" peaches

Pistacchi di Bronte—Bronte pistachio

Provola dei Nebrodi—cow's-milk cheese

Provola della Madonie—cow's-milk cheese

Ragusano—cow's-milk cheese

Razza Modicana—Modicana cow

Sale Marino artigianale di Trapani—Trapani artisan sea salt

Suino Nero dei Nebrodi—Nebrodi black pig

Vastedda del Belìce—sheep's-milk cheese

SARDINIA

Casizolu—cow's-milk cheese

Pecorino di Osilo—sheep's-milk cheese

Razza Sardo Modicana—Modicana ox

Zafferano di San Gavino Monreale—San Gavino Monreale saffron

ITALIAN ALPINE REGIONS

Mieli di alta montagna—high-altitude honey

The Slow Food International Presidia

(presented at the Salone del Gusto 2002)

ARGENTINA

Yacòn

The cultivation of this Andean root dates back to Argentina's pre-Hispanic period. The plant has a fine stalk with green leaves and grows over a meter high. Andean farmers rotate the yacòn with corn or potatoes, cultivating the plant all year round. The flesh of the yacòn can be eaten raw, after it has been left for a few days in the sun and the skin has shriveled slightly. It has the consistency of a pear, with a light hay-yellow color. The yacòn is an important part of the native diet of the people of Quebrada de Humahauca, in the northern region of Jujuy, who also use it to make candies, jams, and jellies.

ARGENTINA

Andean Corn

In Argentina, the Catamarca province is home to a wide variety of corn types: Capia (reddish or white rounded kernels); Pisincho (tiny pointed kernels); Morocho (with rounded kernels); Amarillo de Ocho (large round yellow kernels); and Chullpi (wide flat kernels). The fields where these varieties are raised are tiny, and the farmers still use ancient tools like the *arados de palos* plow, pulled by mules. Corn is an important ingredient for various traditional Catamarcan dishes such as *tamales*, the classic stuffed corn husks, and drinks, including alcoholic beverages like *chica de maiz*.

BOLIVIA
Andean Llama

In the Incan world, the domestication of native llama species permitted the development of an economy founded on the production of their meat, wool, and leather. The consumption of llama in Bolivia dates back 6,000 years, and the ancient system of drying and conserving llama meat (*charqui*) lives on today. Dried and salted *charqui* is prepared from May to August, when temperatures in the mountains dip below zero. The meat is high in protein, can be stored for long periods of time, and is a fundamental ingredient in the local cuisine. *Charqui* is salty and rich, with spicy and gamey flavors.

BRAZIL
Guaraná of the Sateré Mawé

Guaraná trees bear bunches of red fruits, each single fruit containing three black seeds. They have been cultivated for thousands of years in the Mawè region (today known as Sateré-Mawé) of Brazilian Amazonia. This Presidium promotes the guaranà of the Sateré Mawé tribe, which farms this native fruit in small fields bound by the forest. The seeds of the guaranà contain up to 5 percent caffeine and, after drying in a clay oven and roasting on a fire of aromatic muruci wood, they are used to make a powder. This powder forms the base of various drinks, syrups, and fruit juices.

DOMINICAN REPUBLIC

Jamao Coffee

Jamao is the mountainous zone of Salcedo, the smallest province in the Dominican Republic. In Jamao, small farmers grow bananas, corn, beans, pumpkins, and—above all—coffee. This is an excellent coffee, thanks to the altitude (over 700 meters [1,400 feet]), the hand cultivation, and the avoidance of any chemicals or treatments for the plants. This coffee grows best in the shade, usually at the foot of palm and banana trees. Before roasting, the coffee beans are husked, then left to ferment briefly, washed, and left to dry thoroughly.

GREECE

Mavrotragano

On Santorini—that famous sliver of an island known for its black sand and sunsets—Mavrotragano has always been among the favored grape varieties. In the sandy volcanic soil of the island, the grape escaped the devastating Phylloxera virus, and today it is one of the few nongrafted grape types in all Europe. The wine is produced after nine days of fermentation and a year in oak, and is a typically southern in style: purplish red, opulent, fruity, and highly aromatic. The notable tannins make it excellent for aging.

GUATEMALA

Huehuetenango Coffee

Coffee has been cultivated in Guatemala since 1773, when the plant was introduced by Jesuit priests. Today, the country produces some of the best coffee in South America. The volcanic region of Huehuetenango is naturally well adapted to the production of high-altitude coffee. The beans from this region are of excellent quality, with medium body, bright acidity, and a notable walnut flavor.

INDIA

Basmati Rice

Basmati rice probably originated in India and Pakistan, and it has been cultivated for centuries on the hillsides of the Himalayas. The area of Dehra Dun, in northern India, is especially well known for certain precious local varieties. The cultivation of these varieties is entirely manual, and the harvest and husking is carried out by hand by the women of the villages involved in the Presidium project. Punjab basmati is pale yellow and highly aromatic (ideal for pilaf); Desi basmati has flavors of sandalwood and white flowers; Basmati Todal has slightly balsamic flavors; Kasturi basmati is aromatic with notes of mint and lemon; and the whole-grain Desi Basmati Bamati has an intense flavor and a deep brownish color.

INDIA

Mustard Seed Oil

Cultivated all over India, mustard is especially characteristic of the Indian states of Rajasthan, Uttar Pradesh, West Bengal, Bihar, Jammu and Kashmir, Haryana, Himachal Pradesh, Madhya Pradesh, and Gujarat. For this Presidium, the seeds are dried, then pressed in small community-owned mills, allowing the farmers to profit directly from the sale of the oil. Mustard seed oil has a fundamental role in Indian cuisine and culture. It is lightly spicy, and used to dress vegetables and to fry traditional treats like pakoras. The seeds and the oil are important in the ritual of Hindu marriage, and the April blossoms are used for Basant, the festival of spring.

IRELAND

Smoked Wild Irish Salmon

In Ireland, the tradition of smoking salmon dates back to the ancient Celtic population. The four Irish producers of the Presidium use only wild fish, taken from local waters no more than six miles from the coast. They smoke the salmon with a wise hand, using only traditional techniques and natural ingredients. This is a delicate task; the quality of the salmon is based on the equilibrium among three ingredients: salmon, sea salt, and wood smoke. Smoked salmon is traditionally eaten with soda or brown bread spread with butter.

Adan Buda Rice

Adan Buda (or Bario rice) is native to the plateaus of the indigenous Kelabit people, more precisely, to a region called Bareo in the center of Malaysian Sarawak. The preparation techniques are ancient and tightly linked to the traditional buffalo farms of the region. The buffaloes are part of this ecosystem: they eat the weeds infesting the rice fields, transport goods, pull plows, and fertilize the fields. Bario rice has tiny kernels and is famous in Malaysia for its consistency: once cooked, it is soft and slightly viscous.

Criollo Corn

Mexico is corn's heartland. Ten thousand years ago, the wild plant, which produced tiny, bitter ears, was domesticated here. Today, literally hundreds of diverse types of corn are cultivated in Mexico. However, Mexicans are increasingly reliant on imported hybrid (and often GM) corn varieties—purchasing nearly half of their corn from their northern neighbors. There are innumerable traditional Mexican methods to prepare corn: *atole, tacos, pastel azteco,* and *tamales.* This Presidium brings together producers from the states of Oaxaca and Chiapas to promote *criollo* (native) corn varieties.

Chiapas Coffee

In Chiapas, coffee plants are cultivated in the warmest regions of the Los Altos region. The plants grow in the shade of other plants, such as banana and orange trees. Today, the single producers earn very little: not more than 50 cents for every kilogram of coffee. For this reason, the Cooperative Mut Vitz (meaning "bird mountain") has brought together approximately 500 growers who wish to sell their coffee directly. Theirs is a product of high cost but optimum quality.

MOROCCO

Argan Oil

The argan tree grows exclusively in the south of Morocco, and the oil produced from its fruits is a fundamental ingredient in the Berber kitchen. Women have always been responsible for the production of argan oil, and the knowledge of how to chip apart the seeds, extract the kernels, and press the oil is passed from mother to daughter. Argan oil is intensely golden, and the flavor has notes of hazelnut, with a light toasted aroma. In the Berber kitchen, a few drops are added to every couscous, and the oil is mixed with honey and almonds for a traditional spread.

PERU

Andean Fruit

On the slopes of the Andean Cordillera, there is a huge variety of rare fruit: lúcuma, a small, egg-shaped fruit with an intensely green peel and and orange and floury flesh; cherimoya, with a scaly green peel and a succulent, sweet white flesh; aguaymanto, a berry covered by a fine skin in the shape of a Chinese lantern; and the tamarillo, an ovate fruit colored deep pink (sometimes tending toward orange or red) with sweetly tart red flesh. These fruits have evolved to thrive in the unique ecosystem of the Andes, and can be cultivated with simple techniques, without extensive mechanization or irrigation. The Presidium works with a cooperative of farmers who cultivate a variety of fruits and sell their products directly in local markets.

POLAND

Oscypek

Oscypek cheese has been produced in the south of Poland, near the Tatra Mountains, since the fourteenth century. The cheese is produced in mountain huts during the summer months, by farmers who stamp each form with their family's sign using a wooden mold. Oscypek is a smoked hard cheese, with a dense cooked curd made exclusively from the raw milk of a local sheep breed. It has an unusual shape (similar to a bobbin or reel) and a lightly acidic flavor, spicy and salty with hints of mature chestnut. It is served thinly sliced, accompanied by wine, vodka, or beer, and is also excellent grilled.

SPAIN

Tolosa Black Bean

This tiny roundish bean has a beautiful deep-black color—decorated with a single white dot. The Tolosa black bean does not require soaking and, once cooked, a few drops of extra-virgin olive oil and a pinch of salt transform it into a tasty stew. It has always been cultivated in small fields flanking the Oria River, and the center of production is the Basque city of Tolosa, just south of Bilbao.

SPAIN

Gamonedo

Spaniards in the know consider this Asturian cheese superior to its famous neighbor, Cabrales. Nevertheless, Gamoneda is little known outside of the Asturias. Gamonedo is made from raw goat, cow, and sheep milk. It has a classic cylindrical shape and weighs about two kilograms (4.4 pounds). The crust is whitish yellow with some blue marks, which often work their way into the cheese itself, forming fine blue veins. The curd is white and tends to be crumbly. At about two months, the flavor is milky with lightly musky flavors. At around four to five months, the cheese fully blossoms, becoming creamy with a lightly spiced flavor. In Asturia, it is eaten with local apple cider, the traditional beverage of the region.

UNITED KINGDOM

Artisan Somerset Cheddar

The first written record of cheddar cheese is an entry in the expense book of the royal family in 1170. Today, it is the best-known cheese in the world, although the majority of its production is in the hands of large industry. Presidium cheddar is produced in the county of Somerset in southwest England with the most traditional techniques. The cheese is made on farms with raw milk produced by their own cows, and is worked completely by hand. The production lasts three days and concludes with the wrapping of the cheese in strips of muslin coated with melted lard. The result is a deep and complex cheese with intense aromas.

Slow Food Award Winners

Nancy Jones (Nouachott, Mauritania)—owner of a company processing milk from cattle, goats, and camels that is supplied by nomad herdsmen in the Mauritanian desert.

Nancy Turner (Victoria, Canada)—a university lecturer who has carried out research into the knowledge of Canadian native tribes regarding medicinal and edible plants.

Arturo Chacón Torres and Catalina Rosas Monge (Lake Patzcuaro, Mexico)—two biologists who are working on a project to save the highly prized, but almost extinct *pez blanco*, a fish typical of Lake Patzcuaro and the natural environment that supports it.

Raúl Antonio Manuel (Chinantla, Mexico)—a young farmer who has led his community in reviving vanilla cultivation, thus creating an alternative to the predominant, but economically insecure, cultivation of coffee.

Roberto Rubino (Potenza, Italy)—agronomist and director of the Istituto Zootecnico Sperimentale who founded the National Association for Natural Cheese (Associazione nazionale formaggi sotto il cielo—Anfosc) to safeguard and increase the production of cheese from milk supplied by free-range animals.

Marija Mikhailovna Girenko (St. Petersburg, Russia)—a biologist who has dedicated her life to the research and cataloguing of edible species, directing a department of the Vavilov Institute in St. Petersburg, the third largest germoplasm bank in the world.

Jesus Garzón (Cabezón de la Sal, Spain)—environmentalist and researcher into endangered woodland animals who revived the long-distance transhumance route in Spain from Estremadura to Cantabria, training shepherds and providing the basis for the resumption of this traditional activity.

Roger Corbaz (Prengins, Switzerland)—a phytopathologist who has made a huge collection of local fruit tree varieties that have been almost forgotten. They have great value, due not only to their exceptional organoleptic qualities but also to the potential they offer for investigating resistance properties that have all but disappeared in the commonly available varieties.

Veli Gülas (Çamlihemsin, Turkey)—a beekeeper who breeds Caucasian bees in the forests overlooking the Black Sea in Turkey and produces honey according to traditional methods, using beehives built himself and placed on the branches of trees.

Dal-ko (Dalyan, Turkey)—a cooperative of fishermen that produces *haviar*, the gray mullet eggs salted, dried, and preserved in beeswax following an age-old tradition, which have almost disappeared from the local cuisine and shops.

Alan and Susan Carle (Mossman, Australia)—two self-taught experts who set up the Botanical Ark, a collection of edible plants from rain forests around the world, the environment that is today at highest risk of being destroyed and disappearing.

Graham Harris (Wellington, New Zealand)—senior lecturer at the Open Polytechnic of New Zealand, expert in horticulture and ethnobotany, who has carried out ground-breaking research on the varieties of potato cultivated and used by the Maori people.

American Livestock Breeds Conservancy (Pittsboro, North Carolina, USA)—a semen bank for endangered domestic animal species native to the United States that also offers training and consultancy services to farmers and breeders.

2001 (OPORTO)

Thierno Maadjou Bah and Mamadou Mouctar Sow (Futah Djallon, Guinea)—two agronomists who recognized the vital importance of the néré tree (*Parkia biglobosa*) and set up a project to save the trees and the food ingredient (*soumbara*) obtained from them, thereby protecting and reviving a basic feature of the culture, traditions, and economy of one of the poorest countries in the world.

Amal Cooperative (Tamanar, Morocco)—a women's cooperative that produces argan oil from the kernel of the fruit of the argan tree, a native species that only grows in that region (Essaouira) and whose existence is seriously threatened by drought and intensive exploitation.

Noel Honeyborne (Irene, South Africa)—an animal geneticist specializing in poultry who set up the Fowls for Africa project, which combines the task of saving old breeds with fighting hunger in southern Africa and has made poultry production possible for small farmers, women, and deprived communities.

Carlos Lewis (Coronel Moldes, Province of Salta, Argentina)—an agronomist specializing in tobacco who has been running an agricultural tourism venture for several years. The crops he grows on his *finca* have saved some endangered varieties, at the same time reviving some crafts with poor prospects.

Pablo Jara (Santiago, Chile)—a mechanical engineer who has been pivotal in reviving cultivation of quinoa in Chile. Quinoa is a plant native to the Andean *altiplano*, but it had almost disappeared in Chile. It is a high-protein and energy-rich food, but easy to digest. The revival has significant effects for culture, identity, and economics.

Doña Sebastiana Juarez Broca (Comalcalco, State of Tabasco, Mexico)—a peasant farmer who was a pioneer in the organic cultivation of cocoa with the support of the Asesoria Tecnica en Cultivos Organicos, a nonprofit association. Tia Tana now coordinates three women's cooperatives producing chocolate according to traditional Maya methods.

Adriana Valcarcel (Cuzco, Peru)—a chemistry graduate who runs a company, Mara, producing flour, baked pastries, puffed cereals, and herbal teas based on traditional Andean products that are original and healthy, made of local, traditional ingredients.

Chuyma Aru Association (Puno, Peru)—an NGO (nongovernment organization) that is working to save plant and animal varieties that have almost been lost, reviving contacts among the various communities in the Lake Titicaca region, and endeavoring to save the agricultural knowledge and traditions of the Aymara.

Rew Kuang Choon (Jijuk-ri, Namhae Kun, South Korea)—a fisherman leading a group of around twenty people to maintain a traditional activity, fishing using the *jukbang* method, which literally means "bamboo net." This age-old tradition combines respect for the environment with exceptionally high quality of the final product.

Bija Devi (Dehra Dun, State of Uttar Anchal, India)—coordinator of Navdanya, a project for the preservation and exchange of seeds, who got started in 1990 thanks to the work of Vandana Shiva, world authority in the field of intellectual property rights relating to agriculture, the environment, and small farmers.

Predrag Peca Petrovic (Mionica, Yugoslavia)—a biology graduate who has dedicated his life to discovering and breeding native species, growing rare fruit, and coordinating a project that is the pride of the Yugoslav environmental movement, the Mionica Association of Ecological Research.

Necton (Ria Formosa-Algarve National Park, Portugal)—a company that has saved the old abandoned salt pans in the Ria Formosa Protected National Park, producing very high-quality salt.

Marie-Noëlle Anderson (Geneva, Switzerland)—a healer who follows traditional African methods, she works for the protection of traditional knowledge and the safeguarding of medicinal plants.

The Poppy Growers of Ismailkoy (Ismailkoy-Afyon, Anatolia, Turkey)—Despite the difficulties resulting from NATO agreements on opium poppy production, the small village of Ismailkoy has continued to grow this traditional crop: poppyseed oil was a basic element in traditional Anatolian cuisine but has today almost been replaced by sunflower seed oil.

2002 (TURIN)

Boubacar Camara and Mamadou Bailo Diallo (Fouta Djallon, Guinea)—two individuals who have helped to protect the soungala tree by supporting the production of a drink called *sintin*; this helps the economy of the Fouta Djallon rural communities, protecting the forest from the logging industry and indiscriminate deforestation.

Cauqueva (Quebrada de Humahuaca, Argentina)—a cooperative of 150 farmers that produces local crops, such as potatoes and maize varieties at risk of disappearing, and has created a system that protects an area threatened by depopulation and an endangered culture.

ERPE—Escuelas Radiofonicas Populares del Ecuador (Riobamba,

Ecuador)—a radio station that, in twenty years, has helped thousands of indigenous people to become literate and learn organic agricultural methods. These people now produce quinoa, which they export to create a new source of income.

AMIDI—Asociación Mujeres Indígenas Para el Desarrollo Integral (Pachay Las Lomas, Guatemala)—a women's association that breeds chickens and sells eggs, helping local women to find fellowship and a sense of purpose.

Raúl Hernández Garciadiego (Tehuacán, State of Puebla, Mexico)—Garciadiego has successfully dedicated the last twenty years to improving the lives of the farmers in the Tehuacán Valley. Their main product today is amaranth and their main aim is to reclaim one of the driest areas of Mexico for agriculture.

Asociación K'uychiwasi (Cuzco, Peru)—association that promotes coca leaves as food, producing candies, cookies, and chocolates, thus recovering an ancient and healthy custom of the populations of the Andes.

Dale Lasater (Matheson, Colorado, USA)—By sticking to stubbornly independent and surprisingly successful ideas, Lasater's Ranch in Colorado has shown that keeping animals and land healthy can be economically sustainable. His company, Lasater Grasslands Beef, is giving American consumers an alternative to industrially raised, grain-fed beef, which is demonstrably bad for the health of animals and possibly for the health of the people who eat it.

The American Chestnut Foundation (Bennington, Vermont, USA)—The foundation's aim is to restore the chestnut to the eastern forest and its rightful place in the ecosystem, following a blight that nearly made it extinct. Today it counts 5,000 members in every state (except North Dakota) and nine state chapters within the chestnut's original range, where members actively plant trees and report news back to headquarters.

Katsuhiko Takedomi (Saga, Japan)—a farmer who was a teacher for the first part of his professional life and has recuperated an ancient variety of "colored" rice and succeeded in creating a process of production that is totally organic and takes care of the environment.

UBRA—Uma Bawang Residents Association (Sarawak, Malaysia)— an association carrying forward several productive projects to help feed forest communities and, at the same time, care for the forest by managing a small nursery for some of the most important trees.

Dimitrios Dimos (Avra, Greece)—Dimos has managed to save an ancient indigenous breed—the Katerini cow—from extinction. He is now repeating the process with pigs, sheep, goats, and horses, thereby making a significant contribution to the protection of Greek biodiversity.

Fernando Boucinha Alves (Póvoa de Varzim, Douro, Portugal)— almost the last farmer to keep on using the *masseiras*, a type of natural hothouse dug into the sand dunes that run along the Atlantic coast, which are now seriously threatened and at risk of disappearing.

Haydar Alagöz (Igdir, Turkey)—a farmer in eastern Turkey who has revived an ancient type of apricot in a region left vacant by a century of war. He has succeeded in restoring acres of apricot orchards to the area.

A Chronology of Arcigola Slow Food

1986

May 17–22, Langhe. Though not yet officially constituted, Arcigola organizes the first course devoted to teaching about the wines of Langa.

July 26–27, Serralunga d'Alba, Bra, Barolo. A meeting is held to constitute Arcigola.

1987

November 3. The *Manifesto dello Slow Food* is published in *Il Gambero Rosso*, over the signatures of thirteen personalities from the realms of culture, politics, and entertainment: Folco Portinari, Carlo Petrini, Stefano Bonilli, Valentino Parlato, Gerardo Chiaromonte, Dario Fo, Francesco Guccini, Gina Lagorio, Enrico Menduni, Antonio Porta, Ermete Realacci, Gianni Sassi, and Sergio Staino.

December. The first edition of *Vini d'Italia, la guida al bere bene per esperti e curiosi* (Wines of Italy, the guide to drinking well for experts and those who are curious), compiled by Arcigola Slow

Food and *Il Gambero Rosso*, is published. The fifteenth edition was published in 2002.

1988

April 16–17, Vicenza. The fiduciaries (convivium leaders) of Arcigola gather for the first time; henceforth they will meet annually.

April 29. The first *Gioco del Piacere* (Game of pleasure), a banquet and tasting of wines from around the world, is held simultaneously in restaurants throughout Italy. Arcigola Slow Food has organized the *Gioco* 23 times since, with an average of 4,000 people taking part each time.

July 4, Alba. Arcigola organizes a convention of people from the wine and food business in the Langhe around the topic: "Could the Langa be to Piedmont what the Côte d'Or is to Burgundy?"

November 10–13, Siena, San Gimignano, Montalcino. The first national congress of Arcigola.

1989

June. The *Guida turistica enogastronomica delle Langhe e del Roero* (Wine, food, and touring guide to the Langhe and Roero) is published.

December 7–10, Paris. The International Slow Food Movement is constituted, with the Founding Protocol being signed by delegates from fifteen countries. During this event, the *Almanaco dei golosi* is presented; it is an inventory of Italian foods produced according to traditional methods, compiled by *Il Gambero Rosso* with assistance from Arcigola Slow Food.

1990

Slow Food Germany is constituted.

April–July, Alba. Arcigola Slow Food convokes the "Agrarian Assemblies," twelve gatherings on subjects related to viticulture and wine making addressed by experts from around the world.

November 15–18, Alba. The first international convention on Piedmontese wine, during which the *Atlante delle grandi vigne di Langa, il Barolo* (Atlas of the great vineyards of Langa, Barolo), is presented.

November 29–December 2, Venice. The first congress of the International Slow Food Movement.

November. A new book, *Osterie d'Italia, sussidiario del mangiarbere all'italiana* (Hostelries of Italy, a handbook to eating and drinking the Italian way), is issued by a new publisher, Slow Food Editore. The twelfth edition of this handbook was published in 2002.

1991

June 13–16, Perugia. The second national gathering of Arcigola Slow Food.

November 15–19, Tuscany. The first International Convention on the Wines of Tuscany.

1992

October 12. The Columbus Dinner. Arcigola Slow Food and Legambiente commemorate the discovery of the Americas with 500 dinners in 30 countries. The aim is to gather funds for programs in defense of the Amazon forest and its indigenous populations.

November. Slow Food Editore publishes the *Guida ai vini del mondo* in Italian, French, English, German, and Spanish.

November 12–15, Friuli. International Convention on the Wines of Friuli.

1993

Slow Food Switzerland is constituted.

June 1–7. Arcigola Slow Food organizes the first "Week of Taste," an event (to be repeated for the next four years) aimed at educating the younger generation about food and eating.

June. Slow Food Editore publishes *Il piacere del vino, manuale per imparare a bere meglio* (The pleasure of wine, a manual to learn how to drink better).

November 11–14, Piedmont. The Second International Convention on the Wines of Piedmont.

1994

Slow Food Greece is constituted.

April 8–12, Verona. At the Gran Menu, the gastronomic section of the Vinitaly exhibition, Arcigola Slow Food launches the taste workshops.

September 29–October 2, Palermo. The third national congress of Arcigola Slow Food.

November 10–13, Tuscany. The second International Convention on the Wines of Tuscany.

December 1–4, Milan. Arcigola Slow Food organizes Milano Golosa, the embryo of the future Salone del Gusto.

1995

Slow Food Slovenia, Australia, and Cayman Islands are constituted.

January. The creation of the Tavole Fraterne, aid projects linked to alimentation in parts of the world afflicted with war, dearth, and poverty. The first of these are set up in Amazonia and Sarajevo.

1996

Slow Food USA and Mexico are constituted.

April. The first issue of *Slow, messagero di gusto e cultura* (Slow, messenger of taste and culture), the international magazine of the Slow Food Movement, appears in Italian, English, and German.

November 29–December 2, Turin. The first Salone del Gusto, tentative and modest in size compared to what it would later become, is held; Slow Food launches its project for "An Ark of Taste to save the planet of flavors."

1997

May 5–7, Rome. Under the title "Speaking, Doing, Tasting: Ideas, Projects, and Experiences Regarding Sensory Education," a gathering is held in connection with a series of taste workshops given by Slow Food members in the schools of Rome.

May 10. The first Slow Food Festival is held at Münster in Germany.

June 29. Slow Food publishes the *Manifesto dell'Arca* (Manifesto of the Ark of Taste).

September 19–22, Bra. A meeting entitled *Cheese, le forme del latte, rassegna internazionale dei formaggi di qualità* (Cheese, the forms of milk, an international panorama of quality cheeses) is held for the first time. The format, which will be retained on future occasions, includes a market, taste workshops, excursions for gastro-tourists, social gatherings, and study sessions.

October 16–19, Orvieto. The second congress of the International Slow Food Movement. Discussion is centered on the Ark project, and the preservation of food products at risk of extinction.

1998

Slow Food Japan is constituted.

June 19–21, Rovereto. The fourth congress of Arcigola Slow Food Italia, dedicated to the Ark project and the education of taste, is held.

July 27. At the instigation of Slow Food, the Agenzia di Pollenzo Spa is incorporated, with investors from the private and public sectors; the aim is to restore the residence of the House of Savoy at Pollenzo and install a hotel, a restaurant, a wine bar, and the University of Gastronomic Sciences there.

November 5–9, the Lingotto facility at Turin. The Salone del Gusto is held for the second time, with 52,000 square meters of exhibition space, a market with 354 stalls, 311 taste workshops, 4 halls with special themes, 3 wine bars with 3,000 wines from around the world, 40 social gatherings, cooking and tasting courses, special events, book presentations, meetings, and gastronomic tourist excursions. Attendance is 120,000, with 35,000 participating in the taste workshops. Six hundred twenty-eight journalists are accredited, 243 of them from outside Italy. On November 7, in the context of the Salone, a special meeting of the International Slow Food Movement is held to approve the international constitution.

1999

May. Slow Food launches an appeal in defense of Italy's wine and food heritage, collecting signatures for a petition demanding the revision of the European Union's HACCP (Hazard Analysis Critical Control Point) rules, which are meant to apply indiscriminately to all businesses in the food industry and constitute a grave threat to small-scale artisanal producers.

September 17–20, Bra. The meeting *Cheese, le forme del latte,* is held for the second time.

November. A delegation from Slow Food visits China, where taste workshops dedicated to Italian wine and food are organized.

2000

Slow Food China and New Zealand are constituted.

January. The launch of the project to create Presidia, targeted local projects that aim to preserve and reinvigorate small-scale traditional products that might otherwise vanish. At the October Salone del Gusto, 91 of these are presented.

July. The first issue of *L'Arca, quaderni dei Presìdi* (The Ark, journal of the Presidia) appears.

October. The first issue of *Slowine,* a periodical dedicated to wine, appears in English and Italian.

October 24, Bologna. The first Slow Food Awards for the Defense of Biodiversity are conferred upon thirteen people who have helped to preserve biodiversity in the world.

October 25–28, the Lingotto facility at Turin. The Salone del Gusto is held for the third time, with 130,000 visitors from 80 countries. In the market there are 572 stalls; the taste workshops number 250; 91 Presidia are present; and the number of accredited journalists is 2,000.

2001

January. The Master of Food, a people's "university" of taste, is inaugurated, with twenty courses on alimentary subjects ranging from beer to wine, coffee to spices, and meat to fruit and vegetables.

January 16. The new Internet site www.slowfood.it is launched, followed in April by www.slowfood.com.

May. The number of foods selected for inclusion in the Ark by Slow Food convivia throughout the world reaches 600.

June 1. There are 900 Slow Food convivia active worldwide, 350 in Italy and 550 elsewhere. The most northerly is in Reykjavik in Iceland, the most southerly is in Patagonia (Argentina). There are Slow Food members in 83 different countries.

September 21–24. Cheese, le forme del latte is held for the third time.

Slow Food U.S.A. Today

With more than 10,000 members and counting, Slow Food U.S.A., in a few short years, has become perhaps the most dynamic of the international Slow Food movement's national progeny.

Slow Food U.S.A. has made a clear commitment to developing taste education for schoolchildren whose fast food–saturated cafeterias are the launch pads for future generations of obese Americans.

More than eighty chapters throughout the country have instituted school garden projects, "Edible Schoolyards," vital centers of learning and community, capable of restoring us to a healthier and saner way of living. *Snail* is our U.S. newsletter.

Standardization, industrialization, and other degradation due to "the fast life" threaten our food heritage. Food and nourishment are right at the point where human rights and the environment intersect.

We have joined hands across the sea with 70,000 members in more than 45 countries to publish our award-winning journal *Slow*, the international herald of tastes.

We at Slow Food U.S.A. are dedicated to supporting and celebrating food traditions everywhere by making consumers, that is, parents and children, aware of the richness and diversity of the earth's bounty.

Slow Food U.S.A.
434 Broadway, 6th Floor
New York, NY 10013
Tel: 212–965–5640
E-mail: info@slowfoodusa.org
Web site: www.slowfoodusa.org

Notes

1. APPETITE AND THOUGHT

1. Giovanni Arpino, "Cronaca Piemontese"; from *Il prezzo dell'oro* in Giovanni Arpino, *Opere* (Milan: Rusconi, 1992), p. 290.
2. Giovanni Arpino, "Paese natale," in ibid., p. 314.
3. Ibid.
4. Velso Mucci, *L'Uomo di Torino* (Cuneo: Araba Fenice, 1995), p. 47 (first published Milan: Feltrinelli, 1967).
5. Ibid., p. 48.
6. Ibid.
7. Portinari wrote: "The right to the pleasures of the body is egalitarian; it produces nothing, makes no profit, and is thus free and liberating. On the other hand, it does not take itself too seriously, it appeals to the natural slowness of good sense, and it appeals to the intellectual legitimacy of play. . . . But it does insist, and for that matter guarantee, that fair and honest conditions for the experience of pleasure be created."
8. Mario Resca and Rinaldo Gianola, *McDonald's—Una storia italiana* (Milan: Baldini and Castoldi, 1998), p. 69.
9. Ibid.

2. IN THE BEGINNING, THE TERRITORY

1. For a detailed analysis of the phenomenon of nouvelle cuisine in Italy, see Luca Vercelloni, "La modernità alimentare," in *Storia d'Italia, Annali* 13, *L'alimentazione* (Turin: Einaudi, 1998), pp. 989–993.

3. EDUCATING AND LEARNING

1. As Eva Benelli and Romeo Bassoli write, "There are eight things to eat, including food and beverages, that span the world. Eight products that can be consumed wherever there is a large city . . . hamburgers, pasta, sushi, couscous, Coca-Cola, chili con carne, pizza, and coffee" ("Gli stili alimentari oggi," in *Storia d'Italia, Annali* 13, *L'alimentazione* [Turin: Einaudi, 1998], p. 1014).

4. THE NOAH PRINCIPLE

1. Michel Lacroix, *Le principe de Noé, ou l'Ethique de la sauvegarde* (Paris: Flammarion, 1997).

Select Bibliography

Capatti, Alberto. *L'osteria nuova. Una storia italiana del XX secolo*. Bra: Slow Food Editore, 2000.

Cernilli, Daniele and Carlo Petrini, eds. *Vini d'Italia. La guida al bere bene per esperti e curiosi*. Bra: Slow Food Editore and Rome: Gambero Rosso Editore, 2002. Published annually since 1988. Published in English as *Italian Wines* (London: Grub Street).

Gho, Paola, ed. *Osterie d'Italia. Sussidiario del mangiarbere all'italiana*. Bra: Slow Food Editore, 2002. Published annually since 1990.

Gho, Paola, and Giovanni Ruffa. *Il piacere del vino. Manuale per imparare a bere meglio*. Bra: Slow Food Editore, 1993.

Guida turistica enogastronomica delle Langhe e del Roero. Bra: Slow Food Editore, 2000. First edition: Rome: Gambero Rosso Editore, 1989; second edition: Bra: Slow Food Editore, 1994.

Petrini, Carlo, ed. *Atlante delle grandi vigne di Langa. Il Barolo*. Bra: Slow Food Editore, 1990.

Petrini, Carlo, ed. *Atlante delle vigne di Langa. I grandi cru del Barolo e del Barbaresco*. Bra: Slow Food Editore, 2000. Published in English as *A Wine Atlas of the Langhe* (Bra: Slow Food Editore, 2002).

Petrini, Carlo, ed. *Guida ai vini del mondo*. Bra: Slow Food Editore,

1995. First edition: 1992. Published in English as *Slow Food Guide to the Wines of the World* (Bra: Slow Food Editore, 1996).

Piumatti, Gigi, Piero Sardo, and Cinzia Scaffidi, eds. *Il Buon Paese. Inventario dei migliori prodotti alimentari d'Italia*. Bra: Slow Food Editore, 2000. First edition: 1994.

Nistri, Rossano. *Dire fare gustare. Percorsi di educazione del gusto nella scuola*. Bra: Slow Food Editore, 1998.

Sardo, Piero, ed. *Formaggi d'Europa. Storia, modi di produzione, caratteristiche*. Bra: Slow Food Editore, 1997.

Sardo, Piero, Gigi Piumatti, and Roberto Ruino, ed. *Formaggi d'Italia. Guida alla scoperta e alla conoscenza*. Bra: Slow Food Editore, 1999. Published in English as *Italian Cheese* (Bra: Slow Food Editore, 2001).

Soracco, Diego and Nanni Ricci. *Extravergine. Manuale per conoscere l'olio di oliva*. Bra: Slow Food Editore, 2000.

Index

The translation of this book has been funded by SEPS
(European Secretariat for Scientific Publications).

SEPS

Via Val d'Aposa 7

40123 Bologna

Italy

Telephone: +39 051 271992

Fax: +39 051 265983

E-mail: seps@alma.unibo.it

Web site: www.seps.it